Looking Inside Myself and Surviving

Deliverance from Pain and Embracing Your Purpose

Memoir By: Phyllis M. Ewing

Copyright © 2019 by Phyllis M. Ewing

All rights reserved. In accordance with the U.S. Copyright Act of 1976, the scanning, uploading and electronic sharing of any part of the book without the permission of the publisher constitute unlawful piracy and theft of the author's intellectual property. If you would like to use material from the book (other than for review purposes), prior written permission must be obtained by contacting the author at pewing331@gmail.com or the publisher at admin@iamsherriewalton.com

Walton Publishing House
Houston, Texas
www.waltonpublishinghouse.com

Printed in the United States of America

ISBN#: 978-1-7341214-1-4

Library of Congress Cataloging-in-Publication Data has been applied for.

Some names and identifying details have been changed to protect the privacy of individuals.

Acknowledgements

First, I would like to give honor to GOD for giving me the vision to share my story with the world, as well as the strength and courage to be able to help others along the way that may have or maybe going through similar instances in their own lives. For this I say, thank you.

Thank you to my parents for equipping me with the skills and the knowledge to make it through this journey called life. I love you both so dearly as you will always hold a place in my heart.

To my husband, Dwayne, you are my rock; you have shown me what loving someone is truly about. Twenty-nine years and counting, and I still get butterflies in my stomach every time I see you. Thank you for supporting me and my vision and being patient with me during this journey as I began to bring my story alive. To my daughters Kayla and Taylor, I prayed for you and the miracles came showering down from heaven. I thank GOD every single day for blessing me with you two. GOD really does answer prayers. It is truly a blessing to know what it feels like to love someone more than myself. There is nothing that I would not do for you. To my grandchildren, Ariyanna and Matthew, you guys are my heart and bring so much joy to my life. I couldn't imagine life without you.

To my family and friends, sometimes, I ask myself what did I do so right in my life to be blessed with so much love and such an army of people who have my back no matter what? I love you all from the bottom of my heart.

To my assistants- Stephanie Taylor and Becky Kouame, my book launch team and everyone else who contributed to making this all possible, thank you all so much for working so diligently while helping me pull everything together. I appreciate all the hard work that you have put in making my dream come alive.

To my contributing editor, Mrs. Joyce Lloyd, thank you for being the very first to read and edit parts of my story, for giving me your blessing and the encouragement along the way.

To my photographer, Kristi McMullin, thank you for being patient with me during the photoshoot, you did a fantastic job.

To my publisher, Dr. Sherrie Walton...... we did it. Thank you for believing in me and making my first writing experience a great one. I could not have done it without you.

Table of Contents

	ACKNOWLEDGEMENTS	iii
I	CAREFREE	1
II	FREE SPIRIT	8
III	HIDDEN DESIRES	14
IV	DOMESTIC VIOLENCE & SEXUAL ABUSE	22
V	YES, I DO	37
VI	HEARTACHES AND DISAPPOINTMENTS	46
VII	FINDING GOD	61
VIII	FINDING LOVE	68
IX	WHEN DEATH ARISES	77
X	WHEN MIRACLES HAPPEN	84
XI	DARK PLACES	99
XII	SIMPLY ME	106
XIII	MY PASSION & MY PURPOSE	110
XIV	INSPIRATIONAL QUOTES	114

Phyllis M. Ewing

Make the most of your "carefree" young life as you can.

Anne Frank

I
CAREFREE

This Chapter I Dedicate to my Beloved MeMaw and Pawpaw. You both Are Gone but never forgotten. Rest in Heaven. I love you, and you will forever have a place in my heart."

At the tender young age of seven, I remember playing at my Grandmother's house. MeMaw is what everybody called her. It was a simple three bedrooms and one bath structure home with a white stucco finish trimmed with a black border. The house was secured with black burglar bars around the windows and doors. There were two large chinaberry trees in the front yard and a large open field on one side of the house where we often played tag, kickball, and one-two-three red light. Playing in the big chinaberry trees in her front yard and running up and down the dusty dirt gravel road in the east side of town, are some of my fondest memories. I loved going to MeMaw's house because it had so many trinkets and what nots displayed all over the house. It was layered with red and black shag carpet throughout the house with furniture displaying coordinating colors. There was a huge water cooler air conditioner in the living room window to keep everything nice and cool during the summertime; that was before anyone could afford the updated modern air conditioning units we have today. I clearly reme-mber MeMaw telling the grandkids to go outside and turn on the water hose and spray water on the casing of the cooling unit, which kept the house cooled for a long time, at least until the next morning.

In MeMaw's eyes, I could do no wrong. I got away with a lot of things, which my brother and cousins got whippings for, like wasting kool-aid and staining the kitchen table, leaving the loaf of bread sack open and letting the bread go stale, and for not closing the refrigerator all the way- letting the cold air out. Boy did these things rub MeMaw the wrong way.

Being a child was fun...it was innocent. We spent so much time playing outdoors enjoying the sun and thick green grass. I remember having chinaberry fights and playing in the ditch on the gravel road behind my MeMaw's house, eating wild grapes and raspberries. We would always get into trouble for going to the ditch on the next street over, so we would sneak there anyway while she was doing things around the house and didn't really notice that we were gone from the front yard.

I was the youngest of the bunch, so I got away with a lot more than everyone else. But boy when I got caught doing something wrong, I was so scared. Water would just wail up in my eyes, and then the tears would start to roll down my chubby cheeks. You see, I was "Carefree," so I always thought that I would never get into any trouble. I just continued to do my own thing and didn't worry about the consequences. When we snuck back to the house, we all gathered in the backyard and continued to play. The backyard was like our personal farm. MeMaw had chicken coops, rabbit coops and pig pens that were separated by barbed wire fencing. The grandchildren would always help out with caring for the animals by grabbing buckets and pans and doing the feeding. I was really scared of all the animals, but I tried to act brave around my cousins, so I pretended like I wasn't scared. The smell was something terrible, and it just made my stomach turn. I hated feeding those animals, but I did not dare let MeMaw know that or she would have made me feed them more often.

My grandmother was the sweetest God-fearing person I knew. She believed strongly in the Bible and had a strong Faith in the LORD. She loved going to church and sharing the Word of God with everyone she knew. But, when MeMaw was mad about something that we did, oh boy, look out; she got tough really fast. She would yell out to all the grandkids, "Y'all get your butts in this house, and I mean right now." At the sound of her voice, we would all start running to the front door, falling over each other trying to get in the house before she started calling out to us again. Once we were all in the house, the room went silent; sitting on the beautiful shag carpet, nobody dared to utter a word or even make a sound. As the older people used to say back in the day, "It was so quiet; you could hear a rat piss on cotton", it was just that quiet. She really was not going to whip us; she just sat us down in the living room and talked to us about our behavior and sent us back outside to play. What a relief! Honestly, she didn't have to do much for us to get in line. We all knew she meant business just by the look on her face. He expressions easily said, "don't play with me today because today is not the day".

Who's the Favorite?

I was a happy-go-lucky and very spoiled grandchild and I knew that if anything went down, I would most likely not be the one getting yelled at. I was very carefree, and I believed I could do no wrong in MeMaw's eyes, I felt like I was her favorite. I soon found out that I was not because she had no favorites. She loved us all the same, but for some odd reason, I felt special being the smallest of the bunch.

My grandmother worked for a cookie company, and at the end of the week, the company would let the employees bring home all the leftover cookies. She had an old pickup truck to haul the leftover cookies in. On the weekends the grandkids wanted to stay at her house because we all knew that the cookies were coming. She had all kinds: oatmeal, sugar, peanut butter and chocolate chip. That old pickup truck would hold at least three to four barrels of cookies, and we had a field day eating just cookies galore.

Papaw

MeMaw and our Pawpaw were divorced as far back as I can remember, but they were always cordial to each other- they had nine children together. My Pawpaw lived out in the country, so often, my parents would take us out to visit him. I remember him as a gentle and humble man. He had his share of farm animals too. He raised big pigs, little pigs, wild hogs, chicken, cows and he even raised greyhound dogs. About halfway down the rocky road heading to his house, you could smell the hog pin and slop a mile away; "Whew"! The smell was so horrible, and if you just had eaten supper, you would get sick to the stomach. I really didn't like going to the country that much, simply because I couldn't stand the smell and most of the time it was always a muddy mess and I wasn't sure if I was stepping in mud or animal poop. I wasn't an animal lover, but my brother JC and cousins were. They loved being out in the country in the Summer breeze and just running wild, oh but not me, I tried to stay in one spot simply because I didn't want to step in any poop or mud. I guess you could say I was a kind of a prissy little girl, didn't want to get anything on me, no animals, no mud and definitely no poop.

Papaw had a great passion for raising and racing greyhound dogs also. Some weekends we would all go to the dog races at the county dog track. We would sit there anxiously waiting as the greyhounds were lining up at the gates, ready for the handlers to release the jackrabbits. Once the rabbits were released and began running down the long dirt track, the greyhound dogs were released out the gate running full speed ahead down the track, closing the gap as they approached the rabbits. Some of the dogs caught their prey, and some got away. The purpose of the dog race was to see which dog could run the fastest-the rabbit was the bait. All that mattered to the judges was how fast each dog was and how well they were trained, and of course the winner received a prize, and the owner collected a trophy. That was how I remembered my Papaw. He enjoyed the simple things in life.

I have great memories of the times I spent with my grandparents. I will never forget their legacy.

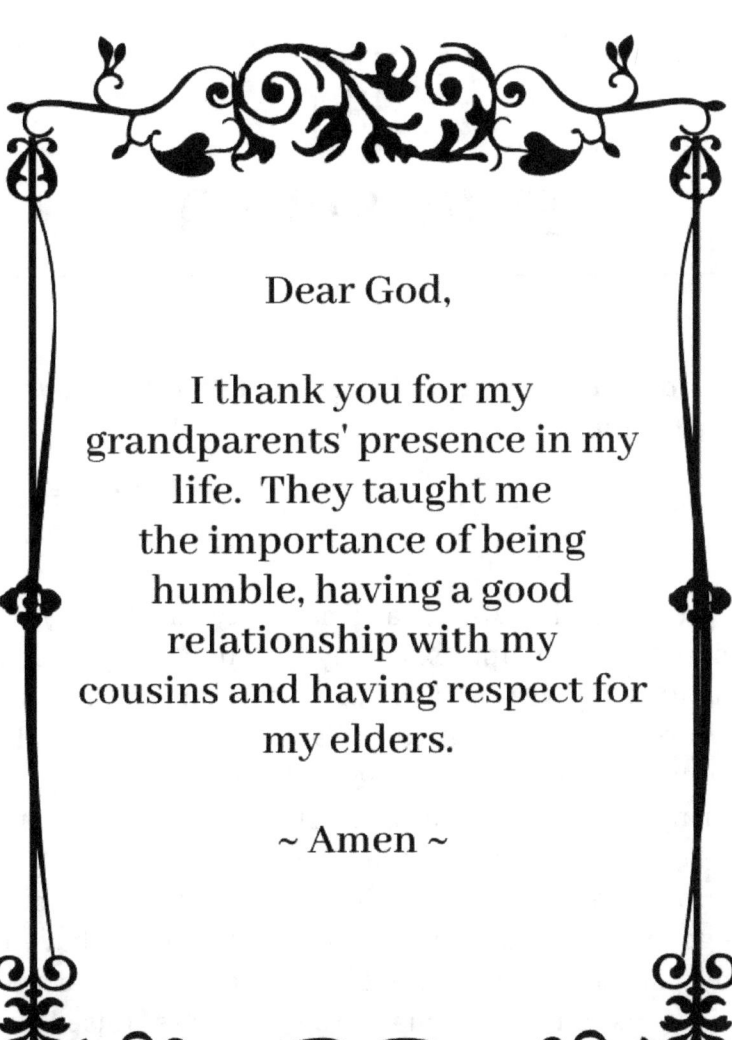

Dear God,

I thank you for my grandparents' presence in my life. They taught me the importance of being humble, having a good relationship with my cousins and having respect for my elders.

~ Amen ~

II

FREE SPIRIT

"I like to be a free spirit. Some don't like that, but that's the way I am."

— Princess Diana

I grew up in Waco, a small city in Texas with a population of approximately 130,000 people, standing halfway between Dallas and Austin on the Brazos River. Waco is the birthplace of comedian Steve Martin, Dr. Pepper (the soda company) and home to Baylor University. I grew up during the time in the late sixties and early seventies when most African American people didn't have much money or resources to have the finer things in life, but they made good with what they had. My family didn't have much, but my parents did the best they could to provide a loving home for us on their small wages. I was raised on the eastside of town in the Estella Maxey Projects (EM Projects). On every block there were large green, and brown dumpsters overflowing the curbs with discarded items as the cool breeze sent some of the trash swirling through the air into the surrounding neighbor's front yards. It was a tough neighborhood mostly made up of African American low-income families and the elderly. I don't know if people had much hope for better lives, but they did support one another. Even in their poverty there was always a sense of community. As a matter of fact, many people like myself grew up and still call Waco home 'til this day.

The streets were always filled with people hanging out on the corners, just shooting the breeze. You could hear the laughter of happy kids running up and down the paved sidewalks playing chase or hopscotch. Some kids played on their worn front yards running in and out of the water sprinklers in and across interrupted flower gardens. Other kids played in the parking lots throwing rock pebbles across the empty parking spaces.

As a child, I would ride my bike up the block, turn around and back down the block as the wind blew through my short afro puffs. "Wee, Wee", I yelled out as I passed by some of the elderly people sitting on their porches. If I was not riding my bike, I was sitting on our front porch playing pickup jacks by myself. I didn't fit in with the other kids, although I wanted to make friends my age. I never knew why I was so shy around other people, but I was. I was just different somehow.

Like the other kids in the neighborhood I enjoyed playing pickup sticks and four squares. Four squares required two people and sadly to say I didn't even have two friends. When I attempted to make new friends, an awkward feeling flowed through the pit of my stomach, and suddenly I felt sick. Those years were very lonely for me.

I Am a Free Spirit

Free Spirit: A person who thinks and acts in an uninhibited way without worrying about normal social rules. Merriam Webster Dictionary

If I had to use a word to describe myself, it would be free spirit. I am an easy-going person, and I don't judge or second guess one's individual character. Over the years I have fought desperately to find myself as I sorted out my individualism. I also learned to be respectful of others and their choices.

"Free Spirit": I am an individual with a unique attitude and lifestyle with an infinite imagination with an outsider's individualism; in other words, I just didn't fit into anyone's circle. Growing up, I was a stay-to-yourself kind of person, a loner. I did not bother anyone, and I did not want anyone bothering me.

Being Bullied

As I approached middle school, I remember the other kids picking on me because I was always too afraid to stand up for myself. If anyone asked me for anything, I would give it freely without hesitation for three reasons. First, just because I was an extremely nice person, secondly, I was a scary cat and thirdly, I surely did not want to get beat up by anybody, so I did whatever it took to avoid it all. The kids picked on me and labeled me as an outsider, which made me a very easy target for major meddling and bullying. There were days while riding the school bus home; kids would kick at me, hit me and call me names. They figured that I was not going to say or do anything anyway, so this became a common occurrence- they taunted me all the time.

I didn't fight back. I would often just get off the bus holding back the emotional pain I felt. As I walked about a block and a half to our apartment from the bus stop, I tried to hold back the tears, but I couldn't. The tears rolled down my cheeks- I couldn't hide how I felt. I just hoped none of the other kids saw me crying. If one of them had followed me and caught me crying, I would have made more trouble for myself. The short walk seemed like two hours, but in reality, it was only fifteen minutes.

As I made it to the front porch, I put on my pretend face. I couldn't let my parents know that I had been crying if they had caught me, I would have been in big trouble. My parents always taught me never to let anyone get on my soft side, to be tough and to stand up for myself. But, little did they know, I was the total opposite of a strong girl. Quite honestly, I really didn't know how to stand up for myself and be that tough individual that they always wanted me to be. When I reached home, I went straight to my room (that I shared with my older brother JC) and just laid across the bed silently crying. A silent cry is a type of crying that you do when tears flow down your cheeks, but there is no sound coming out of your mouth.

As a young girl, I struggled with my identity. I would get so upset with myself. *What is wrong with me? Why can't I be tough and stand up for myself? Why do I cry all the time? Why do the other kids in the neighborhood always pick on me?* I often questioned. The bullying started to really affect me. It caused me to be even more withdrawn. When I wanted to ride my bicycle down the sidewalks or in the parking lots, I was often too afraid of having my bike stolen so I stayed inside. I later realized I was not the problem at all; it was the other kids. They were really unhappy kids, unhappy with themselves and who they were as individuals;

they were bullies. I cared about everyone, no matter how mean they were to me. I just didn't understand what would make others treat people so badly. I gave to others who did not have lunch money, I gave to those who did not deserve anything from me, and I gave to those who I knew really needed it. I probably shouldn't have been so nice, but I couldn't help it. I didn't even bother telling my parents about the bullying, because I knew once I stepped on schoolgrounds they couldn't do much to stop the kids from picking on me. I came to the conclusion that crying about it and telling on the other students wouldn't help the situation much, in fact it would only make matters worse because the next time they saw me, they would be extra mean. There was no way of getting out of that, so to minimize the fights between the other kids and myself, I just gave my lunch money, and school supplies up freely to keep from getting beat up.

As the school year went on, I began to realize that most of the kids who were really mean to me were actually outsiders too. They just did not know how to express being that way, other than to be mean and unkind to other people. They were unhappy people from lots of different unhappy places and didn't know how to deal with their inner feelings. They took their hurt out on others. I figured it out, some of those same kids, who are adults now, still do not get it.

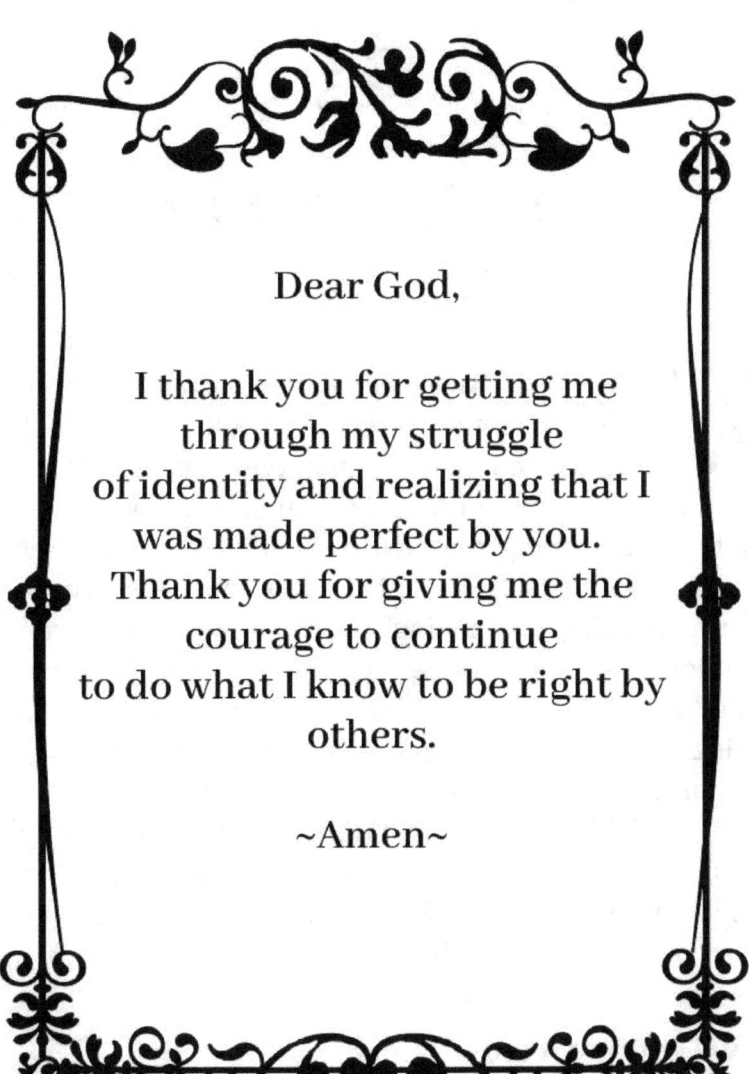

Dear God,

I thank you for getting me
through my struggle
of identity and realizing that I
was made perfect by you.
Thank you for giving me the
courage to continue
to do what I know to be right by
others.

~Amen~

III

HIDDEN DESIRES

We lived in a two bedrooms apartment. At the time it was just my parents, my older brother JC and me. JC and I were just two years apart, so we shared a bedroom with twin bunkbeds with a single nightstand separating the two beds. We shared a dresser, a closet, and a colored TV, which most kids our age, did not have the privilege of having. JC and I were very close. He had a lot of friends. JC would hang out with our cousin Ronnie most of the time, going fishing at Brown Lake or shooting their BB guns. Ronnie was the relative who spent the night every weekend and practically lived at our house, since he and JC were the same age. I did not have any close friends, so I spent my time in our room watching TV, reading, or sometimes playing marbles in the backyard. I kept to myself most of the time.

Early Teenage Years

Late one evening after getting ready for bed while watching TV, I finally fell asleep and was awakened in the middle of the night to Ronnie under my covers and lying on top of me. I said in a grumbling mean voice, "boy if you do not get off of me, I am going to tell my momma on you." He snapped back, "tell her", "she will not believe you...tell all you want, I don't care."

Ronnie kept on violating me and touching my breast and fondling with my private area. I was scared and mad at the same time and I began to cry. I didn't know what else to do but to lay there- I felt so hopeless. The next morning, I woke up and immediately headed to the bathroom. I sat there on the toilet trying to wake up before getting in the shower. It was habit for us to crack the bathroom window to let the steam out from the hot shower, so I sat there with the window slightly open. After about ten minutes, I decided to get in the shower. When I got in, I jumped and was startled to see Ronnie peeping through the cracked window from outside. I rushed and closed the window and the shade, even though the window was only cracked a little, I could just see his eyes squinting through the screen just as I stooped down to rinse my body off. After getting out of the shower and getting dressed, Ronnie was back in the house sitting on the bed watching TV with JC.

"JC", I yelled out, "I am going to tell momma on Ronnie".
JC replied, "What happened, Ronnie, what did you do?"
"I didn't do anything; I don't even know what she's talking about," he replied.
"Yes, I saw you peeping through the bathroom window."
"That was not me; you are lying on me; I have not even been outside this morning."
"Yes, you have, I saw you" I yelled!

The argument went on and on until JC finally said, "Ronnie if you did something, you better tell me right now". "JC, I don't know what she's talking about." He turned and looked back at me "I don't care, go tell your momma, and I bet she won't believe you", Ronnie blurted out. At that point, I felt so small as if no matter what I said it wouldn't have made a difference, because Ronnie was my parent's favorite nephew and JC was their so-called "Golden Boy", they could do no wrong in their eyes. I kept silent about the whole incident.

Weeks went by and Momma decided with our input, to change our room around by stacking our bunk beds. JC's bed was stacked on top. Since I was the smallest, I took the bottom. It actually looked nicer stacked. *Now that JC was on the top bunkbed, Ronnie would not be able to fondle with my private parts anymore,* I thought to myself. I didn't consider since the beds were no longer side by side it would be easier access for Ronnie. Now that the beds were changed, the sleeping arrangements would be Ronnie sleeping on the bottom with me or making a pallet on the floor. All the while, I wished that he would just go home for a change. After a few days went by, and it was time for bed, I fell asleep early. I was awakened by Ronnie under my covers fondling me and squeezing my breasts as JC slept on the top bunk, so again I tried pushing him off of me, but he was too heavy. "Boy get the heck off me. If you don't stop, I am telling". I threatened him again about telling my momma on him. I thought that this dilemma was over with, but man was I wrong.

JC had no clue of what had been going on, so I finally began confiding in him. He questioned me, as if he hoped I wasn't telling the truth. I assured him that it was indeed true, but the look of uncertainty was on his face as he turned and walked away. Ronnie's behavior continued throughout middle school and the beginning of high school.

Not All Bad

Growing up with JC and Ronnie was not always bad. We did fun things like playing board games, playing cards, and we just loved to go out in the back yard and shoot marbles, playing for keeps. We'd count up all the marbles that each of us had won, see who had the most and then go and do it all over again; it was fun.

When I was around 12, and JC was 14, our daddy, who loved the outdoors would take us fishing down at the river and go hunting for jackrabbits in the country, and of course Ronnie just had to come along every time. After fishing, JC and I's responsibility was to clean all the fish that we had caught, that was the only time I remembered Ronnie volunteering to go home because he didn't want to participate in the fish cleaning. We began by laying down plenty of newspapers on the kitchen floor, and the scaling of fish started. Scales were popping everywhere, and then the gutting came next (*talk about stinky*). After that was done, Momma would then take the fish and wash them up really good, wrap them in freezer paper, bag them and in the freezer they went.

Rabbits too!

Not only did my dad catch fish, he caught rabbits also. When it came to the cleaning of the rabbits, I am not sure how momma and daddy took care of that process, because I stayed as far away from the kitchen as possible and at this point, I really don't want to know. After the rabbits were all cleaned and cut up, they were wrapped in freezer paper, and in the freezer they went too.

One day, momma was in the kitchen cooking some good old fried chicken with all the trimmings. We sat down as a family to eat dinner that evening and afterwards, momma said, "Who enjoyed the chicken?" I was the first one to shout out, "Me, Me"! Momma said, "well, I am glad you did because you just ate good old fried rabbit." *What did she say that for?* All of a sudden, I felt sick to my stomach. I jumped up from the table, ran to the bathroom and threw up my dinner. That was the last time I ever ate rabbit. After that day, I would always watch momma in the kitchen whenever she talked about frying chicken. I just wanted to make sure it was chicken and not rabbit.

Mid-Summer- Fourth of July

Every Fourth of July, my family would travel to Houston, Texas, for our family vacation. I would be so relieved because Ronnie couldn't go on vacation with us and I didn't have to worry about him touching me and fulfilling his desires in the middle of the night. I clearly remember my dad driving our car on the ferry, as we moved across the waves to get to my Uncle Milton's large boat. My Uncle Milton had this very large fishing boat that everyone loved to ride on when we all went down to Galveston Beach to swim, fish, and eat BBQ. As I played in the cool sand, I would let it run through my toes as I walked the shore collecting seashells. Later that evening, everyone loaded up on the boat and headed out to the ocean, I held on tight as the cool breeze grazed the softness of my tender face. I was so excited just to be away from home, leaving all the bad memories behind for a week or so, anyway. On the beach and ocean, I had no worries; I felt free for a change.

Looking Inside Myself and Surviving

My Summer Dress

I had my favorite maxi dress that I loved to wear during the hot summer months. My dress was so pretty, and it made me feel like a princess. It was navy blue with yellow flower buds on the top, and yellow with navy blue flower buds on the bottom, a rubber waistband, short puffed sleeves and ruffled bottom. I always wore my white sandals with it. I knew my relatives got tired of seeing me in that same old dress every summer. I realized I was outgrowing that dress and became very upset. I knew that it wouldn't make it to the next summer- it had seen its final days. *What would I wear on the family vacations*? I wondered. I was so perplexed by this that I asked my momma, "Well baby, we will just have to find you something else to wear," she replied. Of course, this was not what I wanted to hear. I frowned with a blank look on my face, feeling disappointed. Vacation ended and it was time for us to return home. After getting home, unpacking, and putting our things away, it was time for everybody to get some rest. While on my bed, I lay there wondering if Ronnie was coming over now that he knew we had arrived back home. I wondered if he would start with those sexual touches again, I was so afraid. My worst nightmare came true and at the door was Ronnie standing there with his overnight bag in hand. "Dang", I whispered, "why couldn't he just stay at his own house for a change?"

Later that night he was under my covers again and I attempted to push him off. "Ouch!" I screamed out as he stuck his fingers in my vagina. My daddy came running in the room. "What's the matter, what's going on"? "Nothing daddy", JC replied, waking up startled. He looked over at me and asked why I was crying. "Nothing I just hit my knee on the dresser that's all", I replied. "Oh okay, well-baby be careful in here", daddy said, as he turned and walked out of the room. Ronnie looked at me and licked out his tongue, meddling, I shot him the finger and covered my head up with the pillow. JC finally told Ronnie, "Hey man, I see you are messing with my sister, you better leave her alone unless you want a big fat knuckle sandwich". Ronnie said, "Do it, JC if you're bad, just do it." "Hey, don't tempt me," JC said pushing Ronnie in the chest. Then Ronnie walked over to my bed and yanked the pillow off my head and said, "told you I would never get caught". "Yes, you will sooner or later because God sees everything", I replied. The many times that I found Ronnie on top of me, although he technically did not have sex with me, he still did violate me.

Right as I was entering high school, I got up the courage to tell momma, and just like Ronnie had warned me, she did not believe me. "It's no way that your cousin would do such a horrible thing" she said. I disputed it, "Yes he did momma." "I do not want to hear anything else about it" she fussed, "he would not dare do such a thing to his own cousin." I stormed out of the room sat on my bed and just cried for hours, which seemed like a lifetime.

Years later, I found out that JC had been beating up Ronnie for doing all those horrible things to me. I never realized that JC was taking up for me all along and had been working on a plan to stop Ronnie dead in his tracks. Finally, JC told momma the truth, and once it was out in the open, Momma gave Ronnie a good butt whipping and sent him home and told him never to come back. Ronnie was now barred from our house for good. At that very moment I had a feeling of great relief because my voice was finally heard by my mother. I had waited for so long for her to listen to my quiet whispers of frustration as I was being violated.

Dear God,

I made it through the chaos by your love and grace. Thank you for opening the eyes of others to bring all the unseen evil actions to light.

Thank you for saving and protecting me from further harm by revealing the unacceptable things that were hidden.

~ Amen

IV

DOMESTIC VIOLENCE & SEXUAL ABUSE

"Anything that works against you can also work for you once you understand the Principle of Reverse."

— **Maya Angelou, I Know Why the Caged Bird Sings**

Entering high school in 1980, I met a guy who I fell head over heels over. His name was Marcus, and he was tall, dark, slim and good looking. I thought he was so handsome. We lived just about a block away from each other in EM Projects, so we saw each other all the time. His sisters, cousins and I all grew up together. As I became older, I tried to fit in more with the girls in the neighborhood. I started hanging out with his sisters and cousins on the corner block. We did what most girls our age did. We would sit there talking, joking around, having fun, laughing and just hanging out. I was a passionate person who cared about people, and I tried to fit in all at the same time. It was obvious there was something different about me. Everybody was always so loud, but I was the quiet one.

Back then I really cared about what people thought about me.

Marcus and I started talking as friends; then as time went on, we became more than just friends. I thought to myself that Marcus just wanted to get into my pants; he knew that I was 16 years old and still a virgin and that I had never had a boyfriend before. He knew that the fast-tailed girls in the neighborhood and some that went to school with us were sexually active, but not me. If my parents ever found out that I was even thinking of having sex, I would have received the whopping of a lifetime. I will admit that I was scared to give up my virginity, so I didn't.

Later that year, we took the relationship a little more serious and officially became a couple. Marcus was a piece of work and a real smooth talker. During our lunch period, we could go off campus to eat, which was a privilege. Every now and then Marcus would buy me lunch, whatever I wanted he gave it to me. He knew how to make me feel special. On the days that we didn't go off campus to eat, we ate in the cafeteria using our free lunch punch cards.

After a while, the oddest things started to happen; Marcus began to act as if he didn't even know me. He stopped joining me for lunch, and I found myself sitting there eating lunch all alone. You're probably wondering if I had any other friends. Well I did, we had mutual friends, but I couldn't depend on them. They were the fair-weather friends- sometimes on and sometimes off. I was okay with being by myself because that is who I was as a person anyway. As time went on, Marcus came around and started walking me to class, and of course, I received the stares from the other girls who wanted Marcus for themselves- because he was so popular. I overlooked all the messy people and went about my business. It was at that moment that I started to second guess myself, trying to figure out if I really wanted to be with the "oh so popular Marcus" and go through all the drama and attitudes from the other girls just because I was his girl. *Was it worth it?* I wondered to myself. I talked myself out of the doubt and convinced myself to stick it out. This was my first real boyfriend, and maybe this is what came with the title, I figured.

Everything about him was so cool. He gambled a little with the other schoolboys, so he had some money on the side. He often gave me money too- putting a little change in my pockets. Eventually I started visiting Marcus quite often at his parent's apartment, about a block up the street from where we lived. He came to visit me too, but not as often. My parents were old school and very strict, and they didn't allow us much wiggle room to get into trouble. I was protected from a lot of things. When Marcus came to visit me, we had to sit in the living room to watch TV and talk, we were never left unattended. My daddy always had his spot at the dining room table, smoking his Benson and Hedges Menthol cigarettes and drinking his favorite beer 'Old Milwaukee sitting 'there listening and watching everything. My momma would be in the kitchen cooking or doing things around the house. My parents really didn't care for Marcus and they felt that he wasn't a good person for me. I thought different of course, but my opinion really didn't matter to them.

It was a different scenario at Marcus' house. Whenever I went to visit Marcus at his parents' apartment, they welcomed me with open arms and told me to make myself at home. Marcus and I watched TV in a room that his parents turned into a den. The first time we did this, I was so nervous, I was shaking; I had never been alone with a boy before. Marcus glared at me and saw that I was nervous and asked if I was okay "Umm …yeah I'm okay" I responded. This must have been a signal for Marcus to make his move because before I knew it, his hands started moving slowly up my thighs and he started caressing my breast. I panicked. *Oh God, what is he doing?* I held my breath until I could hardly breathe. Kissing me with his soft lips touching mine I began to exhale. He proceeded to massage my "salad bowl", and my temperature began to rise, my body was hot all over. In the heat of the moment my body wanted to give in, but my mind kept telling me otherwise. My mind was racing; all I could think was do not get caught up in the heat of the moment. I exhaled again and pushed him away. I was not ready.

Several days went by before I went to visit Marcus again. One day after school, I finished my homework, and I decided to walk up the block to Marcus' house. By this time his family was used to me coming and going, so I would just knock and walk right on in. They were just that comfortable with me. Mr. and Mrs. Shaw really liked me, and I really liked them too, they treated me like family. On that day, his parents were not at home, and I just walked right in and down the hallway. To my surprise, there he was, in his bed with another girl. My heart sank! I was so upset that I just ran up the hallway, out the back door, down the sidewalk- the back way to my home and pass the park. Marcus came after me, yelling, "Phyl come here"!!! I just kept running as fast as I could.

He caught up with me from behind and said, "Baby, I'm sorry it won't happen again". I felt bad and was so weak-minded that I fell for what he said and believed that he was sincere. Two weeks later it happened again with another girl, and I did the same thing, out the back door, down the sidewalk passing the park. And just like the time before he ran after me and gave me the same old story. I fell for it again, feeling bad- as if I had done something wrong. This cycle continued for a while. I was humiliated at school as I faced Marcus, his friends and the many girls that he was sleeping with. Because I wouldn't sleep with him, he punished me by sleeping around. It was as if he was sending me a message, "if you don't want to have sex with me, someone else will." I didn't know what to do; I was so in love.

The next day on the school bus, Marcus came and sat beside me and acted as if nothing had happened. I just sat there in silence. Finally, he said, "What's wrong?" I responded with an awkward look on my face, "Nothing, nothing's wrong Marcus". He looked back at me with a stupid grin on his face and had the nerve to say while bumping me with his arm, "girl you know I love you, you're mine." I sat there thinking to myself, "yeah right me and everybody else". My thoughts were interrupted by the stop of the bus. The bus ride was over; we had made it to school. As we exited the bus, he started touching on my butt, and I told him to stop. He responded, "Stop? Girl you're mine, I don't have to stop." I looked at him and said, "okay Marcus stop, I mean it." He kept disrespecting me, "girl you're mine, I can do whatever I want to do to you."

We went through the school day, but I didn't talk to Marcus at all until lunchtime. On the bus ride home, out of the blue, Marcus started talking bad about me saying that I thought I was better than everybody and too good for him. He told the other kids I wasn't s***. I couldn't believe how badly he was humiliating me. I was so angry with him. Deep down inside, I already knew why he was treating me like this; it was because I wasn't having sex with him. I had my morals, and I wanted to remain a virgin until I found the right person and got married. I was in such a difficult position.

The Rainy Day

After that incident on the bus, Marcus called that weekend and asked if I could come and see him. I was reluctant, but my love for Marcus made me do some crazy things. I asked my mom who surprisingly said "yes", and I proceeded to his house. As I walked down the sidewalk, so many thoughts began to dance around in my head. I had so many questions. *Why would I want to be with someone like Marcus Shaw after he had just humiliated me on the bus?... Why did I let him embarrass me repeatedly? ...Why did I love him so much?* As I approached the front porch, he was sitting there waiting on me, and we both walked inside to his bedroom. "Hey handsome," I said. Out of nowhere, he started yelling and cursing at me saying "you made me look bad in front of my friends." He was referring to the drama on the bus; the drama that he created himself. We began to argue, "Marcus wait what did I do? I didn't do anything wrong it was all you, you made yourself look bad" I told him. He threw me down on the bed and began choking me. I couldn't breathe. I was swinging my arms and kicking my legs trying to get him off me. He finally let up after I picked his fingers away from my neck and my fragile skin. I jumped up and ran out the back door, down the sidewalk passing the park. Marcus turned into a complete maniac as he ran after me. He caught me by my shirt and pulled me backwards. Bam...down we went, slamming to the concrete pavement. I yelled, "Marcus stop, I didn't do anything, he responded, "shut up b****." His eyes stared into mine; he had the look of pure evil. I was so scared; I was crying, and my body was shaking. My heart pounded with fear, and I wondered if the nightmare would ever end. Little did I know that it had just begun. He started kicking me in the stomach; my back, my legs, and then proceeded to punching me all over. All I could do was yell for help, curl up, cry and grunt with every blow from his feet kicking me and his big fists punching me. I continued to cry out, "Stop, please, stop! Why are you doing this to me? I don't deserve this: Why? Why?" "Shut up b****; don't be talking back to me! You won't even give me any p****." You're nothing but an ugly a** whore," he screamed. I was in so much pain, I could barely move, but I finally gained my composure, got up as fast as I could and ran home, limping, hurting and crying from all the physical and mental harm I endured.

When I made it home, momma asked, "What happened to you?" As I began to tell her about the incident, she became so angry I could see the steam coming from her ears as she started grumbling and mumbling in disbelief. I prayed that momma wouldn't tell my daddy because it sure would have been a bigger mess than it already was. My brother JC overheard momma and I talking about the incident and just frowned and said, "that's okay I'll deal with Marcus since he wants to hit girls, let's see if he'll hit me. I'll knock his a** out, and I won't think twice about it." "JC just leave that situation alone, momma said, and Phyl, I want you to stop seeing Marcus; I just knew that it was something about him that I didn't like." I just stood there all banged and bruised up with a blank look on my face. I went to take a bath then got ready for bed. By the time daddy made it home I was already in bed asleep. That was a day I will never forget.

The next morning was Saturday. I was so sore from the beat down that occurred the day before, I really didn't feel like doing much of anything, so I stayed around the house all day. Later that day I went outside and sat on the front porch, and watched the people and cars go by. After about an hour of sitting out there taking it easy, I saw Marcus coming down the street. I was so nervous that I jumped up from the porch and ran in the house. As he walked up the sidewalk and, on the porch, my heart just dropped as I started to sweat. He passed our front door and went upstairs to the neighbors' house whom he was good friends with. I decided to stay in the rest of the day because I knew that he was still near.

As the weekend came and went, I knew I would have to face him as we headed back to school on Monday. When it was time to head to the bus stop, I was so nervous and afraid. I made it down the street as the bus slowly approached and then came to a complete stop. I took a deep breath. As the doors slowly opened, I quickly stepped on the bus and sat near the bus driver- that's where I felt I would be the safest. The next stop was Marcus'. As he got on the bus, he walked past me and said "yeah ugly a** b*****;" I flinched a little but didn't utter a word. I was so scared thinking that he was going to hit me right there on the bus, but since I was sitting so close to the bus driver, he kept walking to the back of the bus.

As the days went on, we saw each other in the school hallway. He walked up beside me and started apologizing for all that he had done and said to hurt me. I just kept walking as the palms of my hands began to sweat from being nervous. My heart was beating fast; I knew all the evilness and the physical hurt that he was capable of. I tried to keep my distance as much as I could. As I walked away from him, Marcus yelled out real loud down the hallway, "Phyl! I love you girl." I suddenly stopped in my tracks. It seemed as if the world began to move in slow motion as if everyone was focused on what all the yelling was about. I was so embarrassed. After he stopped making a scene, some of classmates began to tease me saying that I was in love with Marcus and I just couldn't deny the fact that I really was despite all the hurtful and harmful things that he had done and said to me. It was true. I really did love him, or maybe I really didn't know love at all.

Senior Year

It was 1984, my senior year in high school and prom time. This was a special occasion we all waited for. Each girl anxiously waited for the boy to ask her to the prom. Marcus asked me to go to the prom with him, and I said yes. I was so excited that he asked me, after all we had been through, he was still willing to be with me.

The Prom

I picked out a long soft pink lace gown to wear. Momma curled my hair in spiral curls and added just a little bit of makeup to my face; I felt so beautiful. Marcus arrived on time to pick me up, driving his daddy's pickup truck, and off to prom we went. I was so excited that I was going on a "real" date. Even with my midnight curfew I felt like a grown-up. My parents made sure to enforce my curfew time and warned me that if I were one minute late, I would be in big trouble. I really didn't like the fact that I had a curfew. Marcus could stay out as late as he wanted and I was afraid that since I had to be home early, it would give him time to mess around on me. Unfortunately, there was nothing that I could do about that; nothing but be home by midnight. My parents wouldn't have it any other way...their house... their rules.

It was no surprise that even on prom night Marcus was disrespectful to me. We only danced together twice the entire night. The rest of the time he was having fun with his friends and dancing with all the girls. Sad and disgusted, I sat there on the bleachers by myself. I was fuming, mad and sweating bullets at this point. Once he got tired of dancing, mixing and mingling with everyone, he finally made his way back to where I was sitting. "Hey baby, do you want some punch?" he asked. I gave him a dry response; "yeah punch is fine". He could barely look at me and concentrate on what I was saying because the whole time his eyes was wondering around the room; then we went to take pictures. I should have known that this night would be a repeat of the last few dances we attended together. The homecoming dance, earlier in the year, was a lot worse. I remember my mom dropped me off and picked me up and we didn't take pictures at the party. The Valentine's dance was the same scenario, but at least I did take pictures by myself and with an upper classmate, which was nice.

After taking prom pictures, Marcus had a change of heart. "You want to dance"? "Sure, why not?" I replied. We hit the dance floor. I was surprised that he even wanted to dance with me considering everything he had done that night. Even though I was his prom date he didn't act like it- and for some reason I settled with that. I took a glimpse down at my watch and realized that it was getting close to my curfew time. I knew that I had to be home by midnight, so we left the dance and headed home. The night had finally come to an end.

The New Ride

As Graduation was approaching Marcus' parents gifted him with a car. I was happy for him despite all the abuse he had put me through. Quiet as it was kept, I also thought that since I was his girlfriend, I would get to ride around with him. It was just what I wanted to prove he was all mine finally, and I could make all the other girls jealous. When it came time for school the Monday after the car was presented to him something happened. Marcus didn't show up to pick me up. I feared he must have been in an accident or something tragic occurred, so I caught the bus to school. When I arrived, I saw Marcus was already there with his crew at his side. He just glared at me without speaking one word. The bell rang, and everyone began to move to class. After that mornings' incident, I told him that maybe we should just call it quits. It was clear that he didn't want to be with me because there were other girls in the picture; he agreed. Soon after that, I saw him walking another girl to class, all hugged up, and of course I was hurt, really hurt, holding back the tears; I just kept walking.

My mind was rambling all over the place as I began to ask myself, *why do you continue to put up with Marcus and his mess?" Why do you constantly let him hurt you, physically and mentally?* I did realize that to some degree this was abuse, but I was young. My heart did more leading than my mind did. My heart was shattered in a million pieces. I just couldn't seem to shake him. I was so in love with him, and I thought he loved me too; but not the same kind of love I had for him.

After two months went by, we started back dating again. Throughout the whole relationship, Marcus kept abusing me physically and mentally, and it was really wearing on me.

Being young and naïve and believing that I was in love, I stayed with him through all the mess; talking down on me, calling me names, hitting me upside the head and pushing me down. He started accusing me of cheating on him and that added another bump in the road. Love is all I had to go on to stay with him. When I love I love strong and hard, and that is what I was hanging on to. Deep in my mind I knew that Marcus was not good for me, but I just wanted that feeling of being loved and wanted by someone.

I Gave Away My Innocence

I allowed the fear of losing Marcus to the other schoolgirls to influence my decision to have sex with him. This was my last hope and desperate plea to keep him from messing around on me- so I hoped. We set the time and the place outside of our parent's houses. We met up at six o'clock in the evening at one of his friend's house for that special moment. I was scared, but I followed through with it knowing that finally we would be alone together. He didn't waste any time going in for the kill. As we began to become intimate, it became very uncomfortable for me. He held me so tight that it hurt, "you're holding me too tight, and you're hurting me, I shouted. I began to cry as he put his hand over my mouth and told me to be quiet. I felt like I couldn't breathe, I suddenly began to hyperventilate; I felt flushed, then sick of the stomach. When he was done, he wiped the tears from my cheeks. "Are you okay?" he asked, "Yes, just uncomfortable," I replied. "I wasn't trying to make you uncomfortable; I just love you.... you'll be okay," he said. Thank God it was over.

Still feeling the pain from the day before I headed to school with the hopes of seeing Marcus. I had finally given him what he wanted, and I couldn't wait to show off that I was all his and he was all mine. He came around the corner with another girl on his arm, and just like that, the person that I gave up my virginity to blatantly slapped me in the face. I couldn't believe what I was seeing. *How dumb was I to give it up while knowing he would probably be trying to get into someone else's pants? Well it's done now, and I can't take it all back, I have messed up big time*, I thought.

Graduation day finally arrived. As our names were called everyone was excited as we each walked across the stage with pride. What a great accomplishment we all had made graduating high school. It was such a proud moment for our parents. My oldest brother, JC, surprised me by flying in from Germany to see me. He enlisted in the army his senior year and left right after graduating. I was so glad to see him considering he hadn't been home in two years. This was a great moment for him to see me walk the stage also. I was full of tears as my heartbeat so fast, "you did it, you made it across" I said to myself. After the graduation ceremony, I went to dinner at a nice restaurant with my family to celebrate my big accomplishment. Later that night would be the neighborhood graduation party given by one of our classmate's mom. I knew that everyone would be there, but at the same time, I wondered if my parents were going to give me the okay to go. So I just blurted it out over dinner, "can I go to the graduation party?" My parents conferred with each other before saying, "yes, but be home by twelve; you still have a curfew." I looked at my watch, wow, I better hurry, I don't have much time. We left the restaurant shortly after and headed home.

When we arrived home, Marcus pulled up and parked in front of my house, but he didn't get out of the car. My parents knew that I would be going to the party with

Marcus, but they weren't big fans of him. However, they respected the fact that he was my date and refrained from putting too much pressure on me and advised me to be careful. Time was ticking, and I didn't have time to change into something a little less dressy, so we proceeded to the party just as we were. We were only there every bit of an hour, just enough time for me to enjoy myself a little. Midnight quickly approached and it was time for me to head home. After turning on my street, Marcus said, "well I'm going back to the party, with sadness in my voice, I said "okay." I got out of the car and went in the house. I went to my room and just sat there with an evil look on my face wondering what Marcus was doing and who he was doing it with. I knew that he couldn't be trusted, but I was so blindly in love and didn't want to face reality. I put my blinders on again. I had been through a lot of heartaches in this relationship, but I conditioned myself to accept his behavior. After that night, I finally confronted him about all the nonsense he was doing, hugging and kissing on the other girls. "Baby I'm sorry, it won't happen again" he responded. He seemed sincere this time, so I believed him again and moved on.

Dear God,

I thank you for allowing me to make it through all the mental and physical abuse that I have been through thus far at such a young age.

Thank you for showing me that my body is sacred, and my heart is gentle and that I need to treat it as such. Thank you for seeing me through high school and crossing the graduation stage with such great joy.
Without you none of this would have been possible.

~ Amen ~

V

YES, I DO

Just a few weeks after graduation Marcus asked me to marry him. I couldn't believe it. I knew that it was probably the worst decision I could ever make, but that's how badly I wanted him. Like many abuse victims, I kept going back even when I knew I shouldn't. I ignored what my mind was telling me as I watched my heart and my emotions take the lead in my decisions. "Yes, I will marry you!" I was overjoyed and scared at the same time. I convinced myself that things would be better because by then most of the abuse had subsided. *Wait, did I just make this decision without speaking to my parents? What in the world are my parents going to think?* I convinced myself that since I had graduated from high school, I was grown, and I could finally get from under my parents' strict rules... and I did.

In 1985 Marcus and I got married. It wasn't anything fancy; in fact, we didn't even have a formal wedding ceremony. We just went to the courthouse and made it happen. This was the happiest day of my life- we could finally be all the way together as husband and wife. A few months went by until we eventually got our own place and things started to happen so fast. Once we moved and settled in, I was the perfect wife; I cooked, cleaned and did everything for him. Life was great.

The honeymoon phase ended abruptly when Marcus came home angry with rage in his eyes one night. I was so afraid to ask him what was wrong, so I just glared at him with fear in my heart, stiff and scared to move. He began to yell about people in the streets doing him wrong and how he was cheated. Before I knew it, everything was a complete mess. Dinner all over the kitchen floor, pots and pans scattered everywhere. I just ran to a corner and sat still with my head and face covered out of fear.

Things just got worse, and the violent beating began with forceful punching and him dragging me through the house by my arms- the pain was unbearable. As we made it to the bedroom, he began ripping off my clothes while holding me down with his manly strength. I couldn't move, I just screamed, but to no avail, no one could hear me or wouldn't hear me. He began to force himself inside me as I clenched my legs closed as tightly as I could. With that came a slap across the face, "b**** open your legs." I yelled out, "No, Marcus, no". Another slap across the face, "I'm not going to tell you again, open your legs." I gave in and just cried out with pain. When he was done, he told me to get up and go clean up the mess in the kitchen.

I did as I was told while he fell asleep. I took a long hot bath that night and I scrubbed my body. I scrubbed as hard as I could. I tried to rub off the layers of invisible dirt- I felt so dirty. I sat there thinking about what had just happened. *I can't believe my own husband just raped me.* I scrubbed until my skin was raw. This wouldn't be the last time. More and more, getting raped became a regular occurrence. I tried to escape, as I was drug across the floor while being constantly reminded that I was his wife and that he could do whatever he wanted to do to me. It was drilled in my mind so much that I believed it.

The next day was a day of relaxation and taking some time for just me for a change. As I lay across the bed, I realized that the room was kind of stuffy and I decided to let up the bedroom window so some fresh air could flow through. As the day went on, it was getting later and later in the evening and Marcus had not made it home yet. By eight o'clock it was dark out, I was fuming at this point and I had had enough, so I locked the screen door and put the deadbolt on the front door so he couldn't get in. As he walked onto the porch and realized that he couldn't get in, he started yelling, "unlock this got d*** door." "No, I don't want you to hit me again," I implied. "Okay, I'm not going to bother you, let me in."

Circling the house, he noticed that the bedroom window had been left up and he pulled the screen off. I ran to the bedroom to try and close the window when he reached inside and grabbed my shirt then my arm in a mad rage. "B*t**, I will break your damn arm if you don't let me in." I began screaming with pain. "Ouch, let go!" "Are you going to open the door?" he screamed. "No!" I yelled. He pulled my arm harder, breaking the skin, and I gave in. "Okay! Okay!" Finally, he let my arm go as I went to open the front door. As Marcus made his way in, still in a mad rage, he began punching me in the stomach, kicking me and pulling on the arm that was pulled through the window. I just doubled over with so much pain. He grabbed me and threw me on the bed, climbed on top of me as I tried to fight him off. To no avail, it just made matters worse; the rape session had begun. I just laid there sobbing, aching with pain, waiting for it all to be over. He finished doing his business, showered, got dressed and left. I was so sore from the rape and beating, I finally got the strength to get up to take a shower.

I scrubbed myself again, trying to get all of him off me- I was physically and mentally drained. At this point, I had finally had enough of the unselfishness, ungratefulness, the domestic abuse and the rape sessions. My grandmother's voice ran through my head. MeMaw had always told me that I deserved better, and she was right. I called my mother, informed her of what had transpired and told I wanted to come home. My mom agreed. I grabbed a few pieces of clothing and personal items, jumped in my car and headed home. Marcus didn't try to contact me for two weeks after all the drama. I was back at home with my parents and I took a few days off work to give my body time to heal and for some of the bruises to go away.

I finally returned to work. At the end of my split shift at the nursing home while I was walking to my car, I saw Marcus sitting in the parking lot with his car running. There he was waiting on me to get off work. I was so scared; I didn't know what he was going to do to me. He began to yell, "Hey Phyl, I just want to talk to you!" I just ignored him got into my car and left. This routine went on for several days. Frightened about what he would do to me, I began to stay late after work night after night until he would get tired of waiting and would just leave. One evening he didn't leave, so I just got into my car and drove off.

The Pursuit

Marcus was in hot pursuit on my trail while speeding through the busy intersection. I turned into the mall parking lot and jumped out of the car and ran inside.

"Help...somebody help me," I yelled. I saw the pay phones in the designated areas and headed straight over to the phones to call my dad. I was stopped short only to realized that I didn't have enough change. Looking around the crowded mall, I zeroed in on Marcus, with anger on his face he was walking fast almost jogging as he was approaching me. I began to run through the crowd yelling, "somebody, please help me". The mall security thankfully appeared out of nowhere. "Ma'am", are you okay?... Ma'am, calm down, are you okay?" "No! My husband is after me!" I responded frantically. The security personnel spotted Marcus and stopped him for questioning. They slowed him up and that gave me time to get back to my car to try and make it to my parents' house before he could catch up with me again.

By the time I got about a mile or two up the road and looked out of my rearview mirror, I saw Marcus catching up to me, right on my trail. The chase was on, as I floored it passing up several cars, driving about 60 mph while changing lanes. I sped through the red light, looked out of my mirror again and noticed that he got caught by the light. I sped away. I knew I couldn't make it to my parents' house, so I decided to make my way to my dad's mechanic shop which was closer. As I pulled into the gravel driveway full speed, my dad came out of the shop. "Why are you driving so fast?" he asked. I began to tell him how Marcus was after me and tried to run me off the road, by then Marcus pulled into the driveway. "Sir, I just want to talk to her that's all." I replied, "well I don't want to talk to you." Marcus began yelling, "I just want to talk to her!" At this point my dad pulled out his pistol and told Marcus, "Son I suggest you leave my daughter alone right now before this thing gets out of hand. By the way, I will be calling your daddy about what you are doing." Marcus backed away and sped out of the driveway.

After an hour of talking to my daddy while trying to calm my nerves, I was so exhausted from all the chaos. I finally decided to head home. After making it home, I began to tell momma everything that had happened. She couldn't believe the whole dilemma. Momma replied, "Just stay away from Marcus before someone gets hurt." After my conversation with momma, I decided to take a shower and turn in for the night. The next day as I was driving to work, I was so nervous, looking around hoping that I wouldn't see Marcus anywhere. Thank God I didn't. As my day went on, all I could think about was Marcus and if he would be parked at my workplace waiting on me to get off work. But as time passed and it was time for me to clock out, I didn't see him at all. Whew! I was so relieved, and I could finally breathe.

As the months passed by, I didn't see or hear from Marcus. This was a good thing because I really didn't want to see him anyway. Early one Sunday morning, I woke up thinking, *why am I still married to this guy?* My love for him was gone, taking into consideration all that he had put me through, I was done! I decided to go the next week and file for divorce. I was fed up and my mind was finally made up.

Dating Again

After six months had passed, I decided to start dating again, but I took it slowly. I had met someone that I liked, and I felt like I deserved to enjoy my youthfulness. We decided to meet up for a date. It was a cool Saturday evening, around seven o'clock when my date arrived to pick me up. We had decided to go see a movie, then dinner. It felt so good to finally have some fun for a change. I was very cautious and guarded the whole night. As our time together ended for the evening, he took me home, walked me to the door, leaned in and gave me a soft kiss on the cheek and said he had a really good time. I began to blush, and I replied, "so did I". "Well, can I see you again?" he asked. "I don't know" I replied, "but I'll let you know real soon". He started to blush as he walked away to his car. As he drove away, I thought, wow, he turned out to be a real gentleman, something that I was totally not accustomed to. While standing in the doorway trying to get my keys out, all hell broke loose. Marcus appeared and started yelling at me,

"Who was that guy?"
"None of your business, go home Marcus!"
"Baby, I just want to talk to you."
"I have nothing to say to you Marcus," I replied
"But Phyl, I love you."
"Sure, you do, but I don't love you."

This exchange happened while I was still trying to get my key in the door. Suddenly Marcus grabbed me. I was between the door and the screened door and began yelling and banging on the door, "momma... daddy... help me!" *Boom, Boom,* I continued to bang on the door. Finally, my daddy opened the door and asked, "girl what's wrong with you"? With my heart racing, I replied, "Marcus is out here and won't leave me alone." My daddy looked out of the screened door and Marcus ran through the stairway of the apartments and ran all the way home. I never saw Marcus again until I gave him the divorce papers. He refused to sign the papers. "I'll see you in court", I replied as I walked away.

Two months later, it was time to go to see the judge for the divorce proceedings. Since Marcus had made up in his mind that he was not going to sign the divorce papers, I really wasn't expecting him to show up at all. But to my surprise he did. Once in the judges' chambers, we were asked by the judge what was our reasons for wanting a divorce. Marcus standing there with a blank look on his face probably wondered what was I going to say. I began to tell the judge that we had irreconcilable differences though out the marriage which also involved domestic violence and sexual abuse, mentally and physically, and that I request that the marriage be dissolved. Ending this union adding upon this request I would like to reclaim my maiden name. The judge looked at Marcus, then at me and said that the divorce was so ordered and granted due to irreconcilable differences, domestic abuse and other entities. We both signed the divorce papers, after which they were stamped by the court clerk. The judge then hit his grovel and said, "this divorce is now dissolved and so ordered by the court."

After leaving the courthouse, I was so relieved that it was finally over, signed, sealed and delivered. This was the day that the weight of the world had been lifted off my shoulders. I had peace of mind and now I could move on with my life. Marcus and I just stared at each other as we finally... finally went our separate ways.

Dear God,

I thank you for allowing me to see the monster for who he was. I thank you for your grace and mercy covering me. Thank you for your presence of love through this wicked ordeal. I thank you for keeping me safe from harm by someone whom I thought truly loved me.

Thank you for giving me the strength and courage to leave a bad situation and not to second guess myself. Thank you for not allowing my parents to give up on me when they tried to show me the right path and I rebelled against them. Thank you God for loving me without judgement. It was you LORD that brought me though and for this I am forever grateful.

~ Amen ~

VI

HEARTACHES AND DISAPPOINTMENTS

After experiencing molestation at an early age, physical and sexual abuse and a failed marriage, I vowed never to get married again. I really didn't know what God's plan was for me, but I knew that it was time for me to just breathe and exhale while taking the next steps in bettering my life. For me this meant taking a year and a half off from everything and everyone and just living and trying to find myself. Before long I started to walk and hold my head up high as a strong black woman. Even through all the turmoil that I had been through, it just made me a stronger person.

A New Start

When I felt the time was right, I opened myself up to the possibility of love. I met Justin; he was a nice looking guy whom I met while hanging out at my cousin's house. After seeing each other several times coming and going Justin asked me out. The first date went well; we just talked and got to know one another a little more. It was a nice date, so nice that I felt alive again. After dinner, Justin asked, "can I see you again?" I wasn't totally sure because I really wanted to take my time with relationships at this point and time in my life, being that I have been through so much in the past. Justin was a gentleman and he didn't pressure me to move faster than I was ready.

We went on our second date a few weeks later. I can't forget that night. It was a cool summer Friday night and the breeze was flowing just right. Justin and I went on a movie date and we both had a great time. Afterwards we went out to eat. We talked and enjoyed each other's company. Now I did notice a small red flag that alerted me while we were out that night. I started to get a vibe that Justin was kind of pushy after he had asked for the second time for a kiss and I told him no. He snared up his nose at me and asked why not. "Because I said so, is that too much to ask of you"? He sighed and said "okay". It was getting rather late, so I decided to turn in early being that I had to get up for work the next morning; considering that I was still living with my parents and they had rules.

After getting home while getting ready for bed, I thought about Justin and how the date went — thinking how I turned him down about the whole kissing thing. *Was I wrong? Was I moving too slow and not being romantic?* I questioned myself. As my mind continued to wander, I thought *well girl you are just being cautious in every aspect and not letting your guard down.* Tired from the night out, I took a bath and went to bed.

Justin and I talked off and on for about six months and things began to get serious- so we made it official. We were an item. He introduced me to his family, they were very nice people. After a while of seeing more of the family and having dinner with them at their home my time at Justin's got later and later. He asked me if I wanted to move in with him and his family. "Well I don't think that my parents would go for that, besides you have not talked to your parents about me moving in, have you?" I questioned. "Let me talk to my parents and I'll let you know." I just knew my parents weren't going to allow this.

He and I decided to ride to Dallas, Texas for the weekend. We checked in the hotel and then took on some shopping. We were having so much fun just enjoying each other's company. We made it back to the hotel later that evening and thought that it would be a great idea to order in. While waiting on the food we set the tone right for the evening with candles lit around the room and the boom box playing slow jams. We began to get all touchy feely with each other while trying to control our hormones. There was a knock at the door, whew!! The food had arrived just in time. We washed up and sat down to eat as we glared into each other's eyes. After we ate, we picked up where we left off and it was so amazing considering that I hadn't been intimate with anyone since my divorce. It was strange but good. After making it back to town, Justin got back on the conversation about me moving in with him and his family. He talked the idea over with his parents', his mother was okay with the idea, but his daddy was not fond of the idea at all. Now the real problem for me was to let my parents in on what was going on and what my plan was. When I broke the news to them, my daddy had steam coming from his ears and didn't say a word. The expression on his face was screaming, *girl are you crazy*? My mom, on the other hand, was not mad but very disappointed in my choices. She felt that choice was a lack of good judgment. I was desperate to move out of my parents' house because they were so strict and moving in with Justin and his family would be just the thing for me to get away.

I made my decision. After three days past, I began to pack a few things to get prepared to move out of my parents' house. Even though my parents were disappointed in my decision, I moved in with Justin and his family. Once I got settled in, it felt weird, I thought to myself, I sure hope this work out and I have no regrets. Justin's mom and sister were glad to have me and welcomed me as I began to unpack and put my things away. His dad was working late so I wasn't sure how this was going to go over with him. Later that evening Mrs. Jones began to prepare dinner, so I offered to help. She said, "oh no baby you are a guest in our home, so just sit back and relax". On the other hand, his sister Meagan said, "You can help me set the table if you like." I replied, "sure I'll be glad to help". After dinner was ready Mr. Jones walked in the front door mumbling something. I was glad to see him, so I spoke with excitement in my voice. "Hello Mr. Jones, how was your day?" He looked at me and frowned and said it was an okay day and walked off down the hallway to wash up for dinner.

As everyone sat down for dinner, Mrs. Jones blessed the food that she had prepared. She had cooked a big southern meal with smothered pork chops, mash potatoes, cabbage and hot water cornbread and some good ole' sweet tea. As everyone began to pass the platter and bowls around the table it was very quiet; so, I figured I would start the conversation off by telling Mrs. Jones how delicious all the food looked and how the aroma and taste was outstanding. After a few minutes passed everyone else began to engage in their side conversations about how their day was. I cleared my throat and replied, "well it was a great day for me too." The room went silent. I wondered if I was talking too much or was it just me feeling some type of way because I was the new person in the house. For the rest of the dinner I just sat there quietly.

After dinner was over, I offered to help Meagan with the dishes as Mrs. Jones put away the leftovers in the fridge. When we finished in the kitchen, Justin and I each took our showers while and relaxed watching a little TV We finally got into bed and snuggled up before drifting off to sleep. The next morning, we both woke up and greeted each other with a warm good morning kiss as we began to get dressed to start our day. Justin went off to work and I was off to school. At the time I was enrolled at a small trade school while working towards getting a secretarial certificate. I also worked in the evening.

Things Began to Change

After about two months of things going great, Justin started to change right before my eyes. His attitude and self-esteem had noticeably declined, and he began to spin out of control for whatever reason. I became very concerned because I knew that I hadn't done anything wrong and was determined to get to the bottom of whatever it was that caused the change in his demeanor.

> "What's wrong with you? You seem down lately" I asked.
> "Nothing, why"? he replied in a rude tone.
> "Ok, look, is there anything that I can do to make things better? I responded.
> "No, you can't, you can't do anything for me".

I sat there wondering what I had gotten myself into this time. I knew that I hadn't done anything wrong to make him act this way. Finally, I just left the conversation alone, considering I didn't want to make the situation worse and I figured that he would work through his issues on his own terms. The next few weeks went by and the same routine except we were having more sex now even though Justin still seemed down at times. I was trying to stay focused because in about a week I would be through with school which would be a big relief off my shoulders.

Graduation

I was presented with a Secretarial Diploma of Completion. I was so excited and proud of my accomplishment. I inhaled...then exhaled and whispered softly, "wow I finally made it!" After the ceremony, I met with my advisors and was offered a job at the local police department as a file clerk. It was a daytime job and it didn't pay much, but I was happy to be employed. I knew that the extra income would benefit me, so I accepted it on the spot. *Wow, I am so lucky? Just what I needed...another job.* I was super excited. I had two jobs, I was a police department file clerk during the day, and I worked at Burger Hutt in the evening. After sharing all the good news with my parents, they told me how proud they were, which meant a whole lot to me considering I was always looking for their approval on life in general. When I told Justin the good news, he finally came around and was not as down as usual and was emotionally excited for me.

That night we were intimate, and it was so amazing I didn't even worry about getting pregnant or anything because I was on the pill, but we were also having unprotected sex, so I knew that there was a possibility. I was so in love that I didn't think about catching a transmitted disease. We were in a committed relationship and I trusted him. The next night it was the same routine once again but this time, something was different. Justin was rough with me that night, so I asked him to stop. "Please stop Justin, you are hurting me." He got so mad he slapped me across my face and told me to be quiet, "You don't tell me to stop" he said. I was in disbelief because I had never seen Justin behave this way. I really wasn't sure what he was so angry about that triggered him to take out his frustration on me. I just laid there with my face steaming from the slap and mad at the same time.

The next day Justin acted as if nothing had happened, but I was still mad at him from the night before. As time went by, the physical and verbal abuse started again and was worse than ever. I was beginning to think that he thought it was okay to treat me this way because it seemed normal to him. I knew it wasn't normal; it was a dysfunction that he had learned, and I endured. I kept accepting his behavior because I was in love and just wanted someone to love me back. The physical and verbal abuse brought back old hurtful memories and opened old unhealed wounds all over again. *I can't win for losing, so what do I do now? Leave, stay, call my parents and ask if I can move back home once again?* I wasn't sure what to do because I loved Justin and I thought that he loved me too; he just had a different way of expressing it. This isn't how love is supposed to be, I told myself, especially with the physical and verbal abuse. This wasn't love at all. It was insane and I didn't want to go down that horrible path once again. I kept bringing the same type of guy in my life. What was wrong with me? Why was every man treating me like this? The relationship became a huge disappointment and caused me heartache. I had to find the right time to talk to him; I had to make a decision.

I'm Pregnant

It was getting harder to talk to Justin and I struggled on whether or not I should leave him. Then it happened. I thought I was pregnant, and I needed to let him know. One night after dinner I told Justin that I needed to talk to him.

> "I think I might be pregnant."
> "WHAT?" he was furious… PREGNANT?… How?"
> "What do you mean how? You were the one who refuses to wear a condom. "
> "But I thought you were on the pill," he shouted.
> "I am, I replied, but the pill is not 100% effective."
> "Well I'll just have to take you to the doctor"
> "Okay I will make an appointment in the morning", I replied.

He walked out of the room and left me sitting on the bed. As I sat there, I tried to compose my thoughts and figure out what my next move was going to be once we checked on this pregnancy.

Dragging myself out of bed the next morning, with my stomach in knots and my nerves jumping all over the place, I dressed for the doctor's appointment; I was so scared. We had to keep it all a secret until we found out what was really going on. The doctor administered a pregnancy test first and it came back positive, I was indeed pregnant. Then he did an ultrasound; smiling the doctor said, "Well Phyllis you are in fact pregnant, but we have a problem". My eyes got big and wide with concern, anxious to find out what the problem was, Justin just sat there with a stupid look on his face. The doctor stated that we had a very complicated issue. "Phyllis you have what we call a tubal pregnancy." Justin and I just looked at each other in shock. "What does this mean?" he asked. "Well it's still kinda early to tell completely just yet so I want you to come back in about three weeks". "Okay, we will see you in three weeks," I responded, and we left.

Three Long Weeks

While waiting on the three weeks to pass, I got to thinking, maybe I should get a second opinion. The next doctor said I wasn't pregnant at all. He told me that I was overly stressed and that I needed plenty of rest. So, what the first doctor said wasn't true at all- I was so relieved. I couldn't wait to tell Justin the good news, considering that we both weren't ready or financially stable to bring a child into this world. Justin responded to the news with an attitude as if the whole dilemma was my fault. I thought to myself, *oh Lord here it comes*;

Whop!! He hit me across my face with a closed fist. I yelled so loudly that his mother came to the door and asked if I was alright. Justin replied, "yeah momma we are alright." "Okay" she replied. I knew that she could hear me crying through the door but didn't want to interfere with what was going on behind the closed door.

It's Over

After that incident, I broke off the relationship with Justin and decided once again to stay single. I eventually moved back into my parents' home. As time went on I worked and saved my mon-ey and went on another journey to discover who I was. I spent some time making new friends and meeting new people.

A New Love

After focusing on me for a while I thought, *let me try the dating thing once again.* I met Robert through a mutual friend. He was nice, funny, good looking and fine as hell. I just couldn't resist him. Our relationship started off very slow and easy. When we met, I was still working hard on myself and my growth and I finally had gotten my own place and moved out of my parents' house. Although I really liked Robert, I couldn't ignore the fact that he had kids. I was not ready for any extra responsi-bilities that could possibly be brought into the relationship, so the fact that he had kids should have been a big red flag for me. I should have taken a step back and asked myself, *Are you really ready to be with a man who already has kids? Are you willing to deal with baby momma drama?* Of course, I didn't pause to make a better decision. My mind was telling me no, but my heart said otherwise. I kept my blinders on and continued in the relation-ship, yearning for love and acceptance, knowing that the outcome could possibly bring more heartbreak- but I continued.

Robert was funny, he made me laugh. It felt so good to laugh again. I should have been thinking about what Robert had to offer other than a readymade family. I should have also paid attention to the signs- he didn't have his own place or his own car. I was not being true to myself about the issues that were blatantly staring me in the face. I just wanted to be loved and accepted by someone... anyone. When I entered this relation-ship I often felt like damaged goods. I felt like I wasn't good enough. My self-worth was so low, and I settled for whatever came my way.

I let Robert move in with me and all his baggage, literally and figuratively. The relationship seemed to fill the emptiness I felt as a single woman. I did my best to keep the sparks flying and he seemed into me also. We did fun things together such as walks in the park, movies, dinner and dancing. We really enjoy-ed being together. He even gave me a promise ring to top it off; I was so excited. We had good times together; I would cook for him and sometimes he would cook for me. We danced to old school music, a lot of cuddling, watching movies and even had a few drinks.

As time went on, I knew what we had seemed too good to be true. Our relationship started chipping away little by little. Devon did not have a car; I started driving him to work. I even allowed him to borrow my car and drop me off to work, while he used the car. This was a big mistake. He really took advantage of the situation and began picking me up late from work. Sometimes he was so late that I had to catch a ride home on several occasions.

Times were good for a while. Until one day, we had a big disagreement and he slapped me. That did it for me, so I thought. I was so blinded by what I thought was for sure love then I found out that I was pregnant. I was so stressed, wondering how I was going to tell my parents. After about four and a half months pregnant, I finally got the courage to tell my parents and it was not an easy task. It was a big disappointment on my part; I felt as if I had let them down, knowing that they wanted so much more for me. I was full of shame and disappointment. Soon after, the doctor put me on complete bed rest, forcing me to stop working until after the baby was born. Since I was not able to work, I had to move out of my apartment. By this time Robert had already moved out and was living with a friend of his. I had nowhere to go. My only option was to move back with my parents, once again, which I refused to do. I contacted Robert and asked if I could move in with him until I was able to get back on my feet and he agreed. Thank God the apartment was furnished, which meant that there was less stuff I had to take with me. I loaded the car with all my belongings- food, clothing, etc. and moved in that same day. When I made it to my destination, I only moved in the essentials. I left all the non- perishable food items in my car until I could come up with a plan of action. Another mistake, while Robert took my car to work and I stayed at the apartment to rest; he took all the food that I had in the car to his other baby mommas' house. I was furious, so mad I began to cry.

Things became worse. At four and a half months pregnant there were more complications and I began to spot blood. I was so scared and didn't know what to do. I told Robert that I was spotting, he replied, "Well hell; go to the doctor on Monday." "Okay," I replied as I drifted off to sleep. I hoped that I would be ok through the weekend. I woke up early Saturday morning, cramping so badly I could hardly move. I had to make the hard decision to call my momma and inform her of everything that was going on. "Just move back home with us, baby," she said. That's all I needed to hear; that reassurance that I would be ok. I could not figure out why I was spotting and cramping; I had kept all my previous doctor's appointments and was always given good reports. One thing that I did find strange at my last appointment was that the doctor could not find the baby's heartbeat, but he assured me that everything was fine.

Finally, the cramping and spotting stopped as I got plenty of rest with my feet propped up as much as possible.

Moving back in with my parents was in my best interest with everything that was going on with the pregnancy. The following week, the cramping and spotting came back hard and heavy. I informed my momma and she told me to keep a close watch on the situation to make sure the pain didn't get worse. Well, it got worse at about two o'clock in the morning. I got up to use the restroom and big clots of flesh began dropping from me; there was blood everywhere. I yelled out, "Momma help!" My momma came running and clearly saw what was happening; she helped me get cleaned up and dressed and off to ER we went.

After arriving at the hospital, the doctors began to run tests, started an IV and conducted an ultrasound. There was still no baby's heartbeat. Then the bombshell exploded. The doctor and nurses came into the room and proceeded to tell me the bad news. "Ma'am, your baby has been dead for about a week from the looks of everything that we see." "What?! No! Tell me this is not happening." "I'm afraid so, ma'am," the doctor replied. "We will have to do a Dilation and Curettage procedure (D&C) tomorrow." I was so upset, stressed, and could not believe what was happening. The doctor went on to explain about the procedure that was going to take place and what the clotting and flesh was. He explained the flesh that was dropping out from me was part of the baby, which had deteriorated inside me. All of a sudden, I could not breathe, my heart started pounding and I began to sweat. Then I just began to cry. I was so hurt, confused and could not understand. I felt as if God was punishing me for all the bad choices that I had made in my life thus far.

The next morning, I had the procedure done, with momma at my side through it all. I did not even think about contacting Robert about it, after all, I was still mad at him for treating me the way he did. Since the move back home he had been missing in action anyway, so what was the point of tracking him down. But somehow Robert found out that I was in the hospital and he arrived after the procedure was done. "Why didn't you call me?" he asked. "I didn't think you cared," I replied. "What do you mean, I don't care, that was my baby too." He walked over to the window and stood there glaring at the blazing sun with his back turned. Finally, I told Robert, "Look; enough is enough, all the hell you have put me through; I'm done." He immediately left the room without saying a word.

Later that day the doctor came by to see how I was doing, so I asked, "What did you do with my baby after the procedure?" He replied, "Well ma'am, it was just a mass of flesh so we could not identify if it was male or female it was too decomposed. We put the mass in a jar, and we will eventually send it off to a university for testing. I started to cry, "you put my baby in a jar!" Feeling hurt, guilty and blaming myself. "Ma'am, I am so sorry, but that is standard procedure. That night I cried for hours until I finally fell asleep. The next morning, momma was there to take me home, at that moment I began to pray to God; that if this is what I have to go through to have children, then I did not want to get pregnant ever again. As I finish this chapter of my life, I have never birthed any children. It still hurts every day. My years were filled with so many heartaches and disappointments.

Dear God,

I am very grateful for Your patience with me and Your presence though so much chaos. I love you for loving me even when I didn't love myself at times.

Thank you for bringing me though once again, through heartache, pain and eventually a loss of life, as part of me will be also lost forever.

~Amen~

VII
FINDING GOD

When you experience the presence of God in your life, it's impeccable. Embrace it with your whole heart.

I was raised up in the Baptist Church and baptized when I was around the age of 12 or so. I have many good memories growing up in my church from Vacation Bible School to the youth retreats, there was always something to keep us busy and out of trouble. I remember those down-home family church picnics too. We had the best picnics with all the good old home cooking that all the church sisters would put together. Easter was another major celebration for us, and we even had real Easter egg hunts. Quite honestly as a child, I really did not know the real meaning of Easter. I just thought it was a Sunday that everybody put on their Sunday's best and went to church and afterwards, all the children would run and hunt for eggs as the Pastor yelled, "Get ready, set, go" and off we went. Afterwards we had a great feast of good home-cooked food at the church. It was not until I got much older that I learned the real meaning of Easter.

In the Baptist Church, I was taken to the pool for baptism with my white robe on and was dipped in the water. I must admit I was scared to death. I couldn't swim, and I just knew that the preacher was going to drop me, so I held on for dear life. As I came up, the water dripped from my ponytails, but I made it through. From the Baptist church, my family joined the Church of God in Christ (C.O.G.I.C.). C.O.G.I.C. was a different kind of church. You could not wear pants to church. On Sundays, most women of the church wore big beautiful hats and beautiful outfits with shoes and handkerchiefs to match. The deacons and the other men of the church were sharp as a tack. The men wore their suede hats with the feather on the side, three-piece suits and shoes to match. Everybody came dressed for a glorious occasion: church and praising the Lord. Our outfits were not all that, but we wore whatever our parents could afford; hand me downs, Goodwill, and McCrory's, which was my favorite store to shop. It felt like we fit right in. It was exciting when we did get a new outfit to wear to church. It was mostly on special days of the year, but we were satisfied with what we had. I still remember what my mother used to tell us, "The Lord says come as you are, and you will still be blessed." You see, the Lord does not have favorite picks. The Lord is all about saving souls not how you look and surely not about the kind of clothes you wear.

During my twenties, I left my childhood faith. In my adult life I didn't like to attend church. I always sensed that you had to go all the time and be involved in a lot of things and eventually that made me not want to go at all. I was living what some would call a non-Godly life. I was going to night clubs, drinking alcohol, smoking and just having a good old time. I was not really into church at the time. I had attended church all the time growing up and I didn't want anything to do with the church or God. As I got older, I backslid (left the faith) picked up some bad habits and made poor choices. I continued partying and doing my own thing. I started hanging out with the wrong crowd, and they were into everything, you name it, they were doing it. Some of the things that they were into, I did not get involved in, I was just anxious, trying to fit in. I loved playing cards for money (gambling) and was good at it. I was smoking cigarettes, marijuana and drinking serious liquor. I was not into excessive drinking or the hardcore drugs, just the mild stuff, but I still knew that it was wrong whether mild or not.

As time went on, I began to question myself *"What in the world are you doing?"* This was not the lifestyle I wanted for myself, so I had to come to my senses and do something about the situation that I was in. *But what?* At the time I did not have the answer, so I just slowed myself down, and

I had to come up with a decision on how I wanted to live my life. I thought to myself, *what about getting back into church?* At that moment, I just sat in my apartment and wondered, *what would be the right thing to do?* A few months passed by, and finally, my mind was made up. It was not as hard as I was making it. All I had to do was just slow all the way down on what I was doing and get my sense of right thinking back on track and *Whola!* The answer was right in front of me all along. I just could not see for all the fog that was clouding my thoughts. The solution to the problem was to get back into church and hopefully find my way back to God. He was the only one who could get my life in order. I knew that I could not do it by myself, and I realized that I needed help from a higher power.

The Prodigal Daughter

Eventually, I went back to C.O.G.I.C. and rededicated my life to Christ. It took everything I had to do that because I was so confused about what to do at the time. Then I heard a voice from God saying, "Come, my child. Let's get it right, and the only way this can occur is that you have to commit and dedicate your life to Me the Almighty, and you will find your way". No more old ways, this was my new beginning in finding God and becoming whole again.

I looked for ways I could get involved now that I had decided to get back involved in the things of God. I tried bible study, but I did not like that. The teaching was too long. Then I joined the choir, well that worked for a little while but, there were too many instructions given. I wanted to do my own thing and that was not happening in the choir. If you were off-key you got yelled at. If someone else made a mistake, we all got yelled at, whew! That was not for me. At the time the Lord was still working on me and I was not quite there yet. Sometimes I would get so mad I could just explode because I was used to doing me. I did not realize that finding God would be so hard and intense. Well, after a few months passed by, I started attending church on a regular basis with my mother and siblings, not bible study or the choir, all that was just too much for me. In Adult Bible Study, I had no clue of what the preacher or teacher was even talking about. For one thing, I did not know the Bible- I was just lost. I wondered why it wasn't like Vacation Bible School (VBS) when I was growing up- talk about fun. I loved VBS when I was a kid. I made new friends and learned new things, did lots of artwork and had dressed up bible play acts for all our parents to come to see at the end of the week. I also used to love when the church traveled out of town to visit other churches, camps, and the good fundraisers we had. Traveling on the old chartered Greyhound buses was the thing to do back then. When it was time for us to go to camp or youth trips, we used the church vans, boy, those were good rides.

Finding my way back was difficult especially dealing with those that were in the church. Sometimes, I felt like I was the world's worst kind of person, so I was really trying to get on God's list to have my soul saved. I had to realize that people could not dictate a Heaven or Hell to put me in, so I finally found God for myself! Wow! It was such an amazing experience. I am so happy I made the decision and stuck with it. He is the Head of My Life, My Beginning and My End, the Alpha and the Omega, The King of all Kings, and the Lord of Lords. He's the greatest Author in the world with the #1 bestselling book of all time, "The Holy Bible". Finding God, it does something to your soul, your spirit, and your self-worth.

I built my personal relationship with Him. I sat back and asked myself, *where had I been all this time*? The answer was... lost. But what is so strange about my whole ordeal is that God was with me all the time through it all. I just could not see through the thick dark clouds that were blinding me. But now I know what a joy it is to know God, Love God, and Worship God who surpasses all understanding. Finding God was an awesome thing. If you do not know Him, you need to get to know Him. Try finding God for yourself, and you will be amazed at how His incredible presence in your life will change you forever!

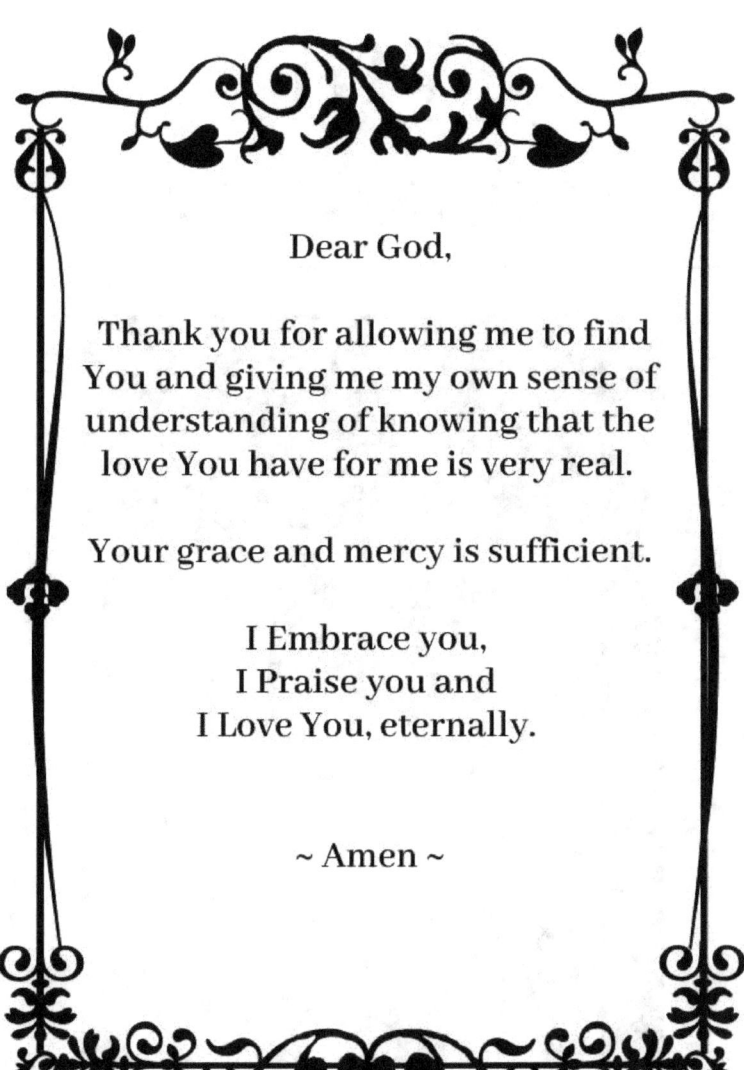

Dear God,

Thank you for allowing me to find You and giving me my own sense of understanding of knowing that the love You have for me is very real.

Your grace and mercy is sufficient.

I Embrace you,
I Praise you and
I Love You, eternally.

~ Amen ~

VIII
FINDING LOVE

Finding genuine love is rare, so when you encounter that emotion, grasp it with great strength, and know that it is something worth holding on to.

Two years had passed since my last relationship. I was single and was not looking for anyone, but God had a bigger plan. A young man named Devin walked into my life. I wasn't sure what his motive was at the time, so I had my guard up. Especially with so many failed and abusive relationships in my past. I met Devin through one of his family members whom we worked with. I was afraid to enter a relationship with anyone and I really didn't trust anyone with my heart because it had been broken so many times before. Accepting him into my life was for me. Even though I desired for a man to walk into my life and sweep me off my feet. I constantly told myself to stop dreaming and that things like that only happen in fairytales, that was not part of my world. I believed that for me finding love was impossible and it wasn't an option. I would often pray to God to bless me with a good, decent and honest man; someone who I could learn to love as my own. Learning to love again was going to be a real challenge for me despite all the negative obstacles that my past brought about. I was afraid of men, afraid of love, I didn't trust men, and I was very unsure about my present and my future. I wanted love, I wanted a good man, someone who would protect me from all harm, love me for me beyond my flaws. Someone to make my smile curl upward with laughter. I wanted someone who I could look toward the future instead of looking back and being reminded of my dark past.

The Perfect Gentleman

Devin was the perfect gentleman. He was tall with brown sugar caramel colored skin and wide broad shoulders, a dimple in his chin with a goatee, which I thought was very sexy. He was a hard worker and so was I; maybe this could work I thought. He was very persistent about asking me out on a date, so after about two months of working together we began phone conversations only. I was very guarded and wanted to move as slow as humanly possible; time was on my side, so I decided to give it a try.

When four months had passed, I decided to let my guard down just a little and decided to give dating another try. So, when Devin asked me again about going on a date with him, I said yes. He gave me the biggest grin as I looked into his eyes and I just blushed with a crooked smile.

Our first date was the movies. We both had our own vehicles, so we decided to meet there. We were not used to seeing each other outside of our work uniforms and we didn't know what to expect. I arrived at the movies a little early and parked and waited. I was really nervous. I looked around as other cars began to pull up, I didn't see his car. Then Devin comes out of nowhere. He wasn't wearing his work uniform, so I wasn't quite sure if that was him. As he approached my car, I realized that it was him, *Wow*. He was wearing starched Levi's, nice crisp button down and some snakeskin boots, *damn, he looked good*. As he walked over, I began to primp in the mirror to make sure my hair was together, and my makeup was on point. I got out of the car. "Wow look at you, you look nice I complimented him". "So, do you", he replied. We entered the theater and took our seats. After the movie was over, we went to a local restaurant, ate, talked and enjoyed good conversation. It began to get late, so we said goodnight and went our separate ways. It was a very good first date. I was pleased.

Months had passed and I was still stuck in my same old routine, work, home, and then repeat. One night after my shift was over, I headed to my car and it wouldn't start. *How embarrassing is this?* I thought to myself. Devin walked over and asked, "Is everything ok?" "Well, no my car won't start." I popped the hood to take a look and check the oil just to make sure I didn't need to add any. "Let me take a look at your oil stick", Devin replied. "It looks like you could use at least a quart of oil." He placed the oil stick back, "try to start it now," he said. "No, that didn't work" I said. I looked under the seat and pulled out a flathead screwdriver. I think it may be my starter, let me give this a try. I placed the screwdriver on the starter and it just sparked. Then I tried it again and it cranked right up. "Wow, where did you learn that?" Devin asked as if he was extremely impressed by my skills. "My daddy taught me that trick just in case I ever got stranded," I smirked. "He taught you very well, now let's go and get that quart of oil. "

We found a corner store to purchase the motor oil. When we went up to the counter to pay, Devin pulled out his wallet, "I got it." "Oh no, I got it…I can pay for it", I replied. "No, I insist, allow me" Devin responded. He was a perfect gentleman. I couldn't believe that he was buying me something. I wasn't used to that. We made it back to the car, put the oil in and I was all set. "I'll call you when I make it home", "ok", he replied, as he got in his car and drove off.

It was eight months later, and our vibes were still going strong. I was working as usual when Devin and one of his friends came through the drive thru. He did something I was not expecting. He surprised me with a big red and white teddy bear and the biggest box of chocolates I had ever seen. It was Valentine's Day and Devin asked me if I would be his girlfriend and I said "yeah, ok". Although my mouth agreed, my mind was still skeptical. I couldn't seem to wrap my head around the idea that someone was taking out the time to do something special for me or even care about me without wanting something in return. Devin was so different.

As months passed, I decided to find another full-time job and just work at Burger Hutt part-time because I wanted my own place. After an altercation with my father, I moved in with my grandmother for a month before getting my own place. It wasn't much, a small one-bedroom, furnished apartment and it was just right for me. About eight months later Devin finally moved in which was a great relief because by him being there just made me feel safer. We were so in love; we did everything together, we were inseparable. For the first time I can truly say that I felt safe and loved, knowing that I had a good man there to protect me from all harm.

After about three years had passed, Devin asked me to marry him, and of course, I said yes. I was so excited and scared all at the same time. Excited because someone loved me enough to marry me and scared because this would be my second marriage and I didn't want it to turn out to be another disaster. I prayed a lot, cried a lot and thought long and hard about the proposal even though I had already said yes. As time went on and everything was still good between us, I couldn't help but be relieved and that I was making the right decision.

In December 1989, we were married, and I just cried with joy. Devin was so excited, he pulled me close and said "Heyyy, we did it". "Yep baby we did", I replied. After the reception, we were off to the honeymoon. We drove down to Austin, Texas the next morning and it was amazing.

Married life was great, the vibes were unbelievable and of course, the sex was outstanding. We were inseparable, joined at the hip, so to speak. I was finally happy for once in my life because I knew that I had someone to hold me at night, protect me from harm, and the one who would have my back and be at my side in spite of all life challenges. He's the one who I gave my heart too and I always knew that he would always be there for me.

After being married a year, we decided to start a family. We were both excited as we began to start the next chapter in our lives. As the months past it began to be disappointment after disappointment because I wasn't pregnant yet. We began to get frustrated and worried because it just wasn't happening for us. All kinds of thoughts popped in my head, *Is it me? Is it him? What's really going on?* As I began to think back about my past and all the beatings that I encountered I wondered if my past was coming back to haunt me and affect my ability to conceive children. *Could that bad miscarriage have put a curse on me?* I questioned. At that moment, all kind of things were going through my mind, and I began to cry. *What if I couldn't have any children due to all the scaring, would Devin still want me? Would this make me feel less of a woman? Would I even be able to handle it all together mentally?* I just didn't know.

Six months later we decided to go to the doctor to get some tests done; we were both scared because we didn't know what to expect and what the outcome would be. After seeing the doctor, we were referred to a specialist. I didn't like the thought of seeing a specialist, thinking all along that something just might be seriously wrong with me, but we made that appointment and followed through with the visit. Upon seeing the specialist, I was nervous as the doctor entered the exam room. He began to talk to us about several different options for getting pregnant and the risks associated. As this long process began to take place, I was starting to question if it was worth going through all the trials and testing.

We wanted a family and remained prayerful and patient. As time went on, I still did not become pregnant. I told Devin that I didn't want to try anymore because I was tired of being disappointed and that the cost of all the testing and doctors' visits were getting rather expensive. We both agreed on the decision to halt the process and explore other options like foster care or even adoption.

As the years passed, I began to fall into a deep depression because I couldn't conceive, feeling sorry for myself. I would feel so broken whenever I witnessed friends and family naturally growing their families. I often asked God, "why me?", "what's wrong with me?" "why can't I have children"? Devin was very supportive and reassured me not to worry and that it would eventually happen for us. He told me we would put our trust in God and be patient. Lord knows I wanted to believe that, but I just couldn't grasp the fact of being childless. I began to pray, "Lord if it's in your will, please bless this union with children, I don't want to go through my whole life without the joy of motherhood. I ask in your name Lord Jesus, let your will be done."

After praying about it, I began to seek advice from my parents. My mother told me, "baby, be still, be patient and be obedient to the Lord and things will eventually fall into place." My father looked at me with a smile encouraging me not to worry. He sat me down and assured me that everything would be okay; he paused for a moment and said, "You know, someday the Lord is going to bless you with a beautiful baby girl, you just wait and see." A few months later my father passed away from cancer and the conversation we had has always resonated with me. I have never forgotten the reassurance he gave me.

Seven years passed as Devin and I put all our time and energy into our marriage and our jobs in the juvenile correction field. All that time had passed, and I began to spiral downward into depression all over again, but I could always count on Devin to be there to get me through the tough times. I knew he was hurting as well but he didn't let that get in the way of helping us get through it all. At this point, we began to do our research about adoption and the foster care system and decided that this was the best option for us. This way we knew we could have a child to raise as our own and to provide a better life for that child. We made that happen as we looked forward to starting a new chapter in our lives.

Dear God,

God, I just thank You for finally placing a very special someone in my life.
Before this, I had prayed tirelessly to be blessed with a good man. I can say, nobody but you God.

You took me through some rough times to be able to enjoy the good times that were coming my way. God, you are so amazing and you have never failed me yet.

I Love You.

~ Amen ~

IX

WHEN DEATH ARISES

Accepting the death of anyone you know is hard, but when death falls within the family, it's a tough pill to swallow. I once asked the question, "how long are you supposed to grieve?" The answer was to grieve as long as you need too, there is no limit. In 1993 when I lost my older brother, due to a car accident, I was so hurt. I had to grasp the fact that he was really gone. My brother was in the military and was stationed in Germany at the time of his death. It just didn't seem fair the way it happened. JC's time was up as an active soldier and he was finally coming home. I was so proud of him and his accomplishments in the military, his life was good. He had called a week before he was going to arrive in the states and told me to pick him up at the airport. When that day arrived, I waited and waited, I was so excited to see him, being that he hadn't been home in about three or four years. Everyone was glad that he was finally coming home. We had no idea what we all were about to experience. It took us by surprise. That day there was a knock at the door. It was the military personnel stating who they were and then proceeded to ask for my parents. My father replied, "Yes Sir, may I help you?" The Officers began to tell my father the sad news. As my mother approached and heard what was being said, she just broke down. Both of my parents began to sob uncontrollably. Upon leaving the officers responded by telling my parents how sorry they were for their loss. Soon after, my mother began making phone calls to many relatives and extended family members and people started to arrive at my parent's house.

My parents didn't know how to reach me, so I was the last to know what had happened. Unaware of the news, I arrived at their house about two hours later and noticed all the cars. I thought he must have made it in and caught the shuttle van from the airport and came on to the city. As I entered the house, I was so excited and spoke to everyone in the room, "Hey everybody". It was quiet, and everyone just looked at me with a blank stare. "What...what's wrong?" I asked. My mother spoke up and said, "Baby, your daddy has something to tell you." "Okay, what's wrong? I asked again. "Where is my brother?" "We just received the news that your brother is dead. He was killed in an auto accident in Germany," my daddy said with tears in his eyes. "No! No! No! He was supposed to call me to pick him up at the airport; this can't be happening." I cried and cried until my eyes were swollen. I was just in shock about it all; in disbelief.

Three weeks had passed as we began to make funeral arrangements for him. We had to wait for the body to be transported from Germany to Dover, Del, where his remains were being prepared before arriving in Texas. We weren't aware of how military funerals was conducted, but we were shocked how military personnel had to be present at all times until the body was laid to rest. We arrived at the funeral home to get the first look at his body for approval, it had already been prepared before being shipped home. It was a very weird feeling. My parents entered the room first and looked at their eldest son as he laid their lifeless. They both began to cry all while trying to console one another as the Military Officer looked on; making sure that no one got too close to the casket. Then it was our turn, the three siblings. I held on tight to my younger siblings' hands as we three approached the room. Upon entering the room, my siblings began to cry uncontrollably as I began screaming out, "No! No! No! You told me that you were going to call me to get you and you didn't". "Why? Why? Lord why?" I began moving closer to the casket as my trembling hands came to a rest on the edge of the casket when suddenly the military officer moved from this stationary spot and said, "Please Ma'am, do not touch the casket or the body". I gave him a look as my eyes darted back and forth around the room as if he was talking to someone else; I just gave a deep sigh, grabbed my siblings' hands and walked out of the room.

After a few days had passed, we were finally finished with the funeral program and set the date and time for the wake and the funeral. As family and friends began to gather at the funeral home for the wake, I became more nervous. The pastor had prepared a short speech, a prayer, a song and then instructed everyone that if they wanted to view the body that they could do so at that time. As different people began to come to pay their last respects, there stood the military officer on guard duty. He stood there watching the movements of everyone, making sure that no one got too close to the body. As I approached to view my brother, I pulled out a small picture frame with my picture in it and proceeded to place it in his uniform pocket and the officer sprang into action; "Ma'am, what is that you have there?" "It's just a small token that I want my brother to have." "Oh okay, I'll take care of it," he responded with his hand out. I handed over the small frame and just walked away.

The next day at the funeral, clergy, friends and family began to arrive at the church. The atmosphere was dim and sad as everyone took their seats in the sanctuary. After the service had begun, my parents began to cry and so did my siblings, but, me, well at that moment, I really didn't know how to feel; other than being sad, I was still in disbelief about the whole ordeal.

Saying Good-Bye to Daddy

Two years later, in 1995, my father was diagnosed with lung cancer. The only thing that I could think of when I got the bad news was *no not again*. We have got to beat this thing. The big C, no one likes to hear that they have Cancer especially if it's unexpected, in which this was the case. I couldn't begin to imagine losing a parent. It was hard enough losing a sibling, but a parent was not an option. I was sad, hurt, confused and mad all at the same time. As time went on, it became hard for my father and eventually, the cancer spread to his throat. He lost all his hair and he began his chemo treatments, then radiation. After about a month of treatments he was given six months to live. The disease was progressing, so we had to try and prepare ourselves for the worst. Within three months, the cancer had spread to his brain and it was moving through his body in the most rapid form. Soon after, he lost his speech, his sight and all motor skills. We were told just to make him comfortable, and that's what we did until the end. My emotions were all over the place. I questioned God about His decision to take my father. I felt that God was punishing me by first taking my brother and now my father. *What was I doing wrong in my life for God to take my love ones away?*

As we prepared to lay my father to rest, it was very hard, but I knew that I had to be the strong one for my Mother and especially for my younger siblings. A military flag was given to my mother for the service that my father had dedicated to the U.S Army. My mother grasped it with open arms and then held it close to her bosom as she cried uncontrollably. It was at that moment I held all my emotions in as I choked back the tears and watched as his casket was lowered.

My Beloved Mother

May 28, 2018 is the day my beloved mother passed away from congested heart failure. This was a hard blow for me to deal with because momma was the glue that held the family together. She was the one that you could talk to when you were down. She was my encourager, my rock, my peacemaker, my prayer warrior, my best friend; she was my momma. The day before she passed, I went to visit her, and we had good conversation and laughter. She was having a little trouble breathing, so I told her not to continue talking, "I'll talk, and you can just listen" I said. She nodded and gave me a sweet smile. Before I left that night, momma told me that she was going to call the doctor the next day because she didn't feel well. "Okay, I replied, just let me know what the doctor says".

The call to the doctor never came. The next morning my mother passed away around 5 a.m. on Memorial Day. When I received the call, I was hysterical, screaming and hollering over the phone. "Oh no, oh no, not momma," I cried out. After hanging up the phone, I immediately contacted my siblings, then my husband. My husband was at work and advised me to stay put and he was on his way to pick me up. As we arrived at mom's house the justice of the peace and law enforcement was already there. They greeted us as we approached the house and said that the body was still in the house and they wanted to know what funeral home they should contact. I gave them the information and was told that the undertakers would let us see her after they cleaned her up. One of my siblings arrived shortly and I gave the update as my other sibling was out of town and we were waiting for her arrival.

When the undertakers arrived at the house, they were directed to the bedroom where my mother lay lifelessly. After tending to my mother, the undertakers informed us that we could see her before they proceed to taking her body to the funeral home. We spent a few minutes before they covered her up and removed her body from the premises. I was so heartbroken, numb and confused. I just couldn't wrap my brain around the fact that all of this was happening.

Later that day, we all met at the funeral home with immediate family coming to see momma before the undertakers removed her for further processing and preparing her for public viewing, funeral service and burial. Picking out her clothing and casket was so hard. My sister made her hair pretty and painted her nails while I did her makeup. I was so nervous, starting and stopping several times until I was done. I must say though, we put our momma away very nice, she would have been proud.

Dealing with Grief

Death is hard for anyone to have to deal with. Everyone grieves differently; it takes some longer than others to get over the death of a loved one. I always advise people to take as long as you need; be sad when you need too, cry when you need to and reminisce as often as you need to. Always celebrate the good times that were shared. Grief is a part of life as we know it here on earth; you go through but eventually, you will get through it with time. Don't be afraid to ask the Lord for peace and guidance during your time of grief. He will always be there to pick up the pieces that are broken. So be patient, give yourself some time, each day, each week, each month and each year will get a little easier.

X
WHEN MIRACLES HAPPEN

Looking Inside Myself and Surviving

In 1998, we were contacted by the State Adoption Agency, informing us about the opportunity of adopting a child. We were so excited to receive the good news that we were going to be parents. The miracle that we had long awaited for was actually happening. Devin and I were so overjoyed upon receiving the good news we couldn't wait to tell everyone. The caseworker met with us, went over all the necessary paperwork, set up background checks, parenting classes, first aid and CPR classes for us both. We took all the required steps it would take to add the new addition to our family including reading a large file with her family history and medical files. Upon setting up a date and time, we went on a visit to a foster home and were introduced to an eighteen-month-old little girl name Kandice. She was so precious with big wide eyes, smooth dark brown skin and a miniature afro. She sat there and stared at us as we approached her with open arms. "Hi Kandice, how are you?" She gave a little smile and continued to play with her toys. Devin reached out to her and she raised her arms for him to pick her up and just laid her head on his shoulder. I just stood by watching with tears in my eyes, tears of joy of course, just to see their first bond. It was priceless. Kandice was rather quiet as she glared at us and I reached out to hold her for the first time. It didn't go so well for me. She began to cry while clinging to Devin's neck. I didn't force her to come to me, but my feelings were hurt. All I could think was *she hates me... she hates me*. Those negative words repeated in my mind repeatedly. I was crushed. How can I become a new parent and the baby hates me already before we even get started? Devin assured me not to worry and that Kandice would come around.

The next three weeks were intense as we prepared everything for our new addition. We had two more initial visits with Kandice at the foster home she was living at, while continuing to create our bond with her before the big move. At our next visit, her hair was not combed and still in the mini afro style and her pamper was soiled. In my mind I was thinking, *what's really going on? Do these people know how to care for this type of textured hair, and they didn't even take the time out to change her diaper?* They loaded her hair down with baby oil and sent her out to play with the other kids that were also in the home. We were allowed to bring Kandice home with us for the next two weekends to get her more familiar and comfortable with us and her new surroundings. Her foster parents packed her a weekend bag and things that she liked to eat. They sent jar baby food and baby milk in which I thought was very strange since she was 18 months old and had a mouth full of teeth. I didn't like the looks of this, so I did something different. After cooking a good hot meal, we went shopping to buy rubber bands, cream moisturizer, hair bows and pull-ups. I began combing her hair, putting it hair up in a lot of small ponytails with colorful bows, she was so pretty, I grabbed the mirror to show her just how beautiful she was, and she gave me the biggest smile and my heart just melted.

When it was time to take Kandice back, they couldn't believe that she was the same child, because she was also dressed nice and her hair was up in little ponytails. "Did she sit still while you fixed her hair? they asked. I replied "yes, she did well". "Wow she doesn't even look like the same child, she's beautiful." "Thank you," I replied. We informed the foster parents about the types of foods Kandice had been eating and they couldn't believe it. However, we could tell that they were not too fond of us giving her anything other than that baby food that they sent. We figured that since Kandice was going to be living with us, she needed to get used to eating regular food not jar food, she was way too old for jar food and baby milk.

The Arrival

It was time for Kandice to live with us. We had decorated her room in the Looney Tunes theme with lots of toys, as we awaited her arrival. We were so nervous, not knowing what to say, do or how to act. This was a new experience for both of us, but we were eager to learn all that we could in order to be the best parents we could be.

When Kandice and the caseworker arrived, she gave Kandice a big hug and assured her that everything would be okay. Kandice then walked over to the caseworker and began to cry as she reached out to be picked up. After showing Kandice to her new room we proceeded with putting her things way. She began to play with the toys until the caseworker said her final goodbye and she eventually drifted off to sleep. Later that day my mother came over for dinner and to meet her new granddaughter. I decided not to give her the baby food, instead I fixed meatloaf, green beans, mashed potatoes, cornbread and sweet tea. We put Kandice in her highchair and placed a plate in front of her. She glared at the plate of food, at me, then back at the plate again. She was looking at the food as if it was foreign to her. My mother picked up the fork and began to feed Kandice and she loved it. Before long, Kandice's plate was clean. The initial visits were finally over and the final visit was here, the next day everyone said their last goodbye's giving Kandice lots of hugs and kisses. Thankful now that the final visit was over, we put her in the car, buckled her down in her car seat and we drove away.

We could finally take time to go shopping for little girl's clothes, shoes and more hair bows, just girl stuff. We didn't realize that there were so many things to choose from and of course we wanted her to have the best of the best. In the meantime, we were discovering other foods that Kandice liked to eat. She wasn't a picky eater and had a very good appetite. Six months later we received a letter from the adoption agency notifying us about our upcoming court date to finalize the adoption. When the time came, we were ready. We put on our Sunday best, Devin wore his nice crisp white dress shirt, black tie, black slacks and Stacey Adams dress shoes. I was dressed in a pink chiffon dress suit and black pumps. Kandice wore a cream colorfully pleated dress, white tights and black patent leather shoes. When we entered the courtroom, there sat the judge, sitting up high on his bench. He glared down at us as we approached the front of the room.

The judge began reading the important criteria for adoption finalization and asked if there was anyone in the courtroom who didn't agree with this adoption finalization. The room was so quiet. I was praying that no one would come forward after all the time that had passed. No one uttered a word and the judge proceeded with his ruling, including changing Kandice's biological last name to our last name, which he granted proudly. Kandice was officially our little girl; we were very proud parents.

The next month one of my best friends gave me a baby shower, even though our baby was already eighteen months old motherhood was still new to me. I was grateful to have wonderful friends. Kandice received so many nice things at the shower. One year went by and everything was great. One day we received a phone call from the State Adoption agency. We were informed that Kandice had another biological sibling in the foster care system and that she had just became available for adoption. They wanted us to adopt her sister as well. We informed the agency that it all sounded great but give us some time to talk things over and that we would be in touch. Devin and I sat down and talked about adopting again which we knew firsthand how the whole process worked. We both had previously decided to raise only one child, but when we got word that Kandice had a sister, we had a change of heart. I couldn't bear the thought of Kandice going through life knowing that she had a sister out there somewhere and that they probably wouldn't see each other ever again.

We decided to inform the agency that we were interested in adopting the sister. Tyhara was five years old with big wide eyes; very light skin, round face and beautiful long ponytails. She was a very pretty girl who wasn't shy about anything. She loved to hug, and she was very talkative. Kandice and Tyhara were two years apart, with two very different personalities. Tyhara had been in the foster care system for some time, but that didn't matter to us. We were only concerned about her well-being and what we could provide for her as parents. As the process began, we went through all the same steps and procedures that we had done previously, only this time it was quicker.

The caseworker set up times and dates for Tyhara to come visit and to meet Kandice. Tyhara always knew that she had a little sister but didn't know what had happened to her. Kandice, on the other hand, had no clue about even having a sibling she was so young. The day that the two finally met was awesome. Tyhara brought Kandice a teddy bear and they both just hugged and giggled. They wanted to go outside to play so we took them to the backyard, and they played on the swing set. They had a blast, running around chasing each other, screaming and just having fun. Devin pulled out the video camera and began to film the beautiful moment. When it came time for Tyhara to leave, she gave Kandice a big hug while trying to pick her up at the same time. Tyhara walked out holding hands with her caseworker Sara as they approached the car. "Are we going to McDonalds Ms. Sara?" asked Tyhara. "Yes ma'am, we are." Tyhara just giggled as Sara opened the door and she hopped in the front seat waving at us as they drove away.

Reuniting Two Sisters

The time had come for Tyhara to move in with us. We were so happy to reunite the sisters and we welcomed her with open arms, just as we did for Kandice. Tyhara grabbed her things from Sara and immediately began putting everything away. She was so excited to finally have a house she could call home. When we went to court to finalize the adoption of Tyhara, we asked the judge to change her biological last name to our last name and it was granted. This completed our family. We had our girls and we had each other. We were truly blessed by God for us to be a great blessing to these two beautiful children.

Meet the Family

During the summertime Devin and I planned a big get together so everyone could finally meet our girls. It was a perfect summer day, 88% with a slight cool breeze. As family and friends gathered at the house, they were excited about the big celebration. There were lots of gifts brought by friends and family along with plenty of food, drinks and games for the kids to play. This bond was the beginning of new friendships for the girls. From that time forward for the next five years or so, I planned the Annual Hot Dog Party for the girls. This was a party where they could invite all their friends, past and present. We would watch movies play games and would have hot dogs, chips and fruit punch to drink. I even had a cake made every year saying, "Annual Hot Dog Day", the girls really enjoyed it.

The year was 1999 and we took our first family vacation together. Devin and I wanted to make this vacation very special, so we planned a trip to Disney World in Florida with the girls.

This wouldn't only be their first vacation but also would be the girls' first time out of the state. The road trip to Florida was going to be a long ride, but we expected to sightsee along the way. We had family in Florida so instead of paying for a hotel for the whole week we were invited to stay with them. They were so excited about meeting the girls for the first time and wanted to spend time with us also, they decided to go to Disney as well.

When we arrived at Disney World, the girls screamed with excitement as they awed over the Disney characters and attractions at the entrance. Once entering the gate and everyone was accounted for, the kids were ready to get wild. There was so much to see and do. The adults had their backpacks loaded down with bottled water and small snacks, a bottle of water cost eight dollars in the park so we packed our own. As we began strolling the park, we let the girls pick and choose what rides they wanted to ride and what games they wanted to play. They thought that was the coolest thing because they were able to make their own decisions.

The Disney Park was so crowded with people, the wait time to get on the rides were long. Every line in the park was long. There were long lines for the rides, the attractions, and even for the restrooms. It was outrageous but the experience was worth the wait. We rode a lot of rides with the girls; Ferris wheel, merry-go-round, carousel and the kiddie roller coaster. There was one water attraction that stood out as most memorable it was called, It's a Small World. It was like a lazy river, but we were in a canoe boat and the scenery was an around the world theme. Every twenty feet or so we were in a different country; there was London, China, United States, Hawaii, Mexico with each having its own heritage with attached flags and colors. It was very pretty and educational.

Later that night there was a stage show then a Disney parade with colorful floats as all the characters marched down the street. The girls screamed in excitement, "Oh wow, look- look... Mickey Mouse...oh look Minnie Mouse!" Devin and I laughed hysterically at how excited they were and just how much fun they were both having. Seeing the joy in their eyes and the laughter on their little faces just made us proud. Our first vacation was such a great success.

Hello Vegas!

It was the summer of 2006, seven years later after our Disney Trip, and the big trip to Las Vegas was finally here. Kandice was now ten and Tyhara was twelve. This time instead of driving we decided to fly, which would save time and wouldn't take away from our vacation days. As we arrived at the airport, our round-trip flights were already booked so all we had to do upon arriving was check in at the ticket counter and check in our luggage. Flying was new to us. We were nervous and excited at the same time. After takeoff, the ride was smooth and before we could get too comfortable it was already time to land. After arriving at Hotel Golden Nugget and settling in we hit the town for shopping and sightseeing. There was a lot to see and so much to do and we were overwhelmed with excitement and didn't know where to begin. Kandice and Tyhara were excited about seeing all the different lights flashing and hearing music that bought the whole atmosphere alive. We walked for hours, just looking at the nightlife, stopping in several shops buying trinkets and gifts to take back home with us. After a few hours of taking in the sights, we headed back to the hotel and turned in for the night.

The next morning, we started our day with a good breakfast before making our way to the main strip, visiting several attractions along the way. The girls began stressing to Devin and me about how much fun they were having and that they wanted to go to Circus, Circus. Okay," we replied, "we'll get there soon". Devin wasn't fond of taking a cab or the shuttle, he was big on sightseeing, so we continued to walk until we made it to the main strip; that was the longest walk ever.

Our first stop was the Mandalay Bay Hotel and Casino. There we took a tour of the shark exhibit, which was pretty cool. Kandice and Tyhara were amazed at the fish, sharks, and baby turtles floating in the tank displayed in an underground cave with a built-in glass aquarium. While we walked through the tunnel, we were able to see everything swimming and floating from all angles. When exiting the main tunnel there was another cave, where you could feed the fish and snapping turtles in the exhibit as the cool mist in the air flowed from the ceiling. Kids of all ages were screaming and running around everywhere with excitement. Upon exiting we stopped at the photo booth for a quick family photo, then we moved on to our next destination.

We arrived at the MGM Grand Hotel, admiring the beautiful decor as we did a quick walkthrough before moving on. The sun was beginning to go down and just down the street was our next stop, Circus, Circus. We made it, just in time for the clown juggling show. Once the girls saw the clowns, the lights and heard the sound of circus music they both began screaming, "Yea, yea clowns...Momma, Daddy...look!" They both yelled out. "We see them," we replied. As the show began, the girls settled down some and focused on the entertainment which lasted about forty-five minutes. After the show we headed upstairs to this huge arcade. Devin and I hadn't seen so many kids and games in one place in our entire lives. Kandice and Tyhara walked slowly, looking all around anxious to start playing games. The air clearly stated Circus, Circus, with the smell of fresh popped popcorn, and the sweet smell of cotton candy definitely had my stomach growling for a long-awaited snack. Devin walked over to the counter and asked the cashier for thirty dollars' worth of tokens, with the girls both on his heels ready to get the tokens in their hands.

As we went from counter to counter playing all sorts of games, Kandice hit it big, winning a huge leopard which stood about three feet tall. It was almost as big as she was. We all were excited about her big win, but the question was," now how are we going to get this huge stuffed animal back to our hotel?" We had to walk all the way back from the main strip to downtown carrying that big thing. Our time on the main strip was over as we headed back downtown with the leopard in tow. It was a long walk back, so we all took turns packing the stuffed animal. Then Kandice began to whine, "I'm tired of carrying this leopard", but Devin and I told her to stop whining and keep walking. Kandice then began to cry, so I took over carrying the leopard for about an hour, then Tyhara carried it for about fifteen minutes, "Momma I'm tired of carrying this leopard", "girl keep walking," I replied. Then Devin took the leopard and carried it for the rest of the way to the hotel.

As we arrived back at our room at the Golden Nugget, we were all pooped, our dogs (feet) were hurting from all that walking; everyone just stretched out on their bed, floor or wherever we could lay down- we were so dog gone tired.

After resting a bit, we all showered and headed downstairs to the hotel restaurant for dinner. After ordering and waiting on our food to arrive at the table, everyone discussed their experiences of the day. It was a hell of a day, but a great one. After eating dinner, Devin and the girls went back to the room and I made my way to the Casino to gamble a little bit. I loved playing the slot machines and it didn't really matter if I won anything or not, it was just the satisfaction of hearing all the money falling out of the machines (back then it was real money in the machines, but now the machines issue tickets) no matter whether it was my machine or someone else's, the sound of money falling was like music to my ears. After winning about three hundred dollars, I decided to turn in for the night and headed back to the room. Everyone was already asleep, so I hit the sack and watched a little TV until I fell asleep.

The next day Devin was up early and headed to the casino, while I stayed with the girls. After everyone was up and ready to start our last day in Vegas, we headed down to breakfast. We planned to have an easy day doing a little more sightseeing and shopping. The day was going by pretty quickly, so we went back to the hotel, packed, and then ate lunch. Later that evening we turned in early for the night because we had to get up early the next morning to get to the airport for our departing flight.

Flying Home

The next morning, we caught a cab and headed to the airport. Upon arriving at the airport while seated in the waiting area Tyhara asked, "Momma, Daddy, are we going home?" "Yes", I replied. "Why do we have to go home?" "Well baby, our vacation is over now. Your daddy and I have jobs we have to get back to." Tyhara looked at me with a frown and her nose turned up and said, "okay", dropping her head down as she turned and walked back to her seat. As we boarded the plane, the girls became excited all over again and we still had this oversized stuffed animal with us. The flight attendant approached me and said, "Ma'am you will have to pay for another seat for the leopard." "What?" I replied. "No problem, we can leave this thing because we are not paying for another seat," I told her. As Devin proceeded to exit the plane and dispose of the leopard in the trashcan, Kandice began to cry. "Girl if you don't hush your mouth about that leopard, we just can't take it back with us," I told her. As other passengers boarded the plane, one gentleman overheard the conversation we had with the attendant and noticed that Kandice was crying and said, "Ma'am, I have room in my compartment to store it for you if you don't mind. "Oh, Okay, thank you so much sir," I replied, "anything for the little one." Kandice looked on with a sigh of relief on her face. "Thank you so much sir," Devin replied. And that's the story of how we made it back to Texas with the oversized leopard and until this day, we still have that mighty leopard that joined our family in 2006 at Circus, Circus, Las Vegas, NV.

Our daughters have grown up to be beautiful, respectful, and smart young ladies. We have given them a great life and the necessary tools they needed to become good productive citizens. We are so proud of them both, their accomplishments in life and the positive choices they have made along the way. We may not be their biological parents, but we are the only true parents that they both know, and we thank God for them every day. We are blessed thus far with two beautiful grandchildren, boy age 7 and girl age 3. They both keep us grounded and are the highlight of our lives. We love them all the same, encourage them in all their endeavors and always remind them to put God first in everything they do and that anything in life is possible because the sky is the limit. We always encourage them to strive for greatness.

XI
DARK PLACES

Sometimes God allows us to go through tough times in order to raise awareness about things that are hidden. Life challenges are not often easy to deal with and it sometimes comes with great doubt about life struggles. Well, I've experienced things in my life that have brought me great heartaches, disappointments and doubt. I often wondered why these obstacles had to come my way, so I began to pray, asking God, "Why me Lord? Why me?" My mother always told me not to question God about what He's doing in your life because God has a plan for all of us. I have experienced many trials in my life that have led me to fall into a deep depression and dysfunction of the mind. Depression is a disease of feeling worthless, having nothing to live for and it can lead to family dysfunction with negative thoughts. The feeling of unworthiness and surrounding yourself with dysfunction and can be very destructive. It will take you to a deep dark place where you may find yourself slipping away from society while losing your sanity.

Family is a bond that can never be broken, but sometimes you must unglue relationships if they jeopardize your sanity. Your mental health is most important, and you must be careful not to let depression creep into your life. My many encounters with dysfunction and depression were within my own immediate family circle with family members that liked to fuss and fight. It's not necessary to take it to the next level, but some do and do it often. When you are physically hit by a parent, that's a major dysfunction; as you are slowly pulled into an already explosive situation of arguments with other individuals and you're the one that ends up getting punched in the face just for being present, that's dysfunction.

When you are sexually abused by a relative and no one believed your outcry, that's dysfunction. When you try to keep peace amongst family, who in their eyes are never wrong about anything, that's dysfunction. When you give your all by helping family when in need and they turn on you for no apparent reason and they believe they are right no matter what the situation is, that's dysfunction. With family, you will forever be bonded in so many ways, but sometimes you have to unglue yourself from them because you can't please everyone and being satisfied with all is not an option.

Depression is the same way; you must unglue yourself from the mindset of all negative energy. Depression will have you so confused that it will flow quickly over into your dysfunction. Depression is an illness that takes control of the mind and with time and great courage anyone can somewhat recover from it. It won't be easy, it's a lot of work and it's a process. It takes great courage to talk about depression and be able to share your experiences with others so that they may learn from your point of view. By sharing your experiences with others you're reassuring them that you can get through some of the struggles. I don't want to make you think everything in my life is totally perfect today. I still sometimes struggle, but I keep pressing forward and I never look back. You may not be where you want to be at this moment, but you are surely not where you used to be and that's a great start.

My depression began when I had many failed attempts and couldn't get pregnant. I so desperately wanted to have children the natural way but was unsuccessful on every attempt. After having some female problems, I eventually had to have a partial hysterectomy, one year later my doctor discovered that I had a thirteen pounds tumor on my left ovary; this led me to have a second hysterectomy. During the procedure the doctors found many small tumors on my appendix and noticed that the large tumor had been bleeding for quite some time. They discovered all my internal organs began to attach to each other including my spine. While in the hospital I contracted a staph infection, which was so bad that I didn't think I was going to make it, so I immediately began to give up. I had lost so much weight, that my face and jaws were sunken in and so fragile. I began sweating badly with fever and the chills. The nurses had to come in several times a night to change the linen, this went on for several days. I was given several kinds of antibiotics and I felt like I was getting worse, so the doctor came in to talk to Devin and me about my prognosis and it wasn't looking good. The doctor proceeded to tell us that she had one more antibiotic to try and that she was hopeful that it would work, but could not give us a guarantee, so basically she was telling me that I was dying and that there was nothing else they could do.

At that moment my heart became heavy and I began to pray, "Lord, I don't want to die, I have my babies and husband to live for." "Lord just take away the pain, heal my body and make me whole again." I turned to Devin and told him that I felt like I was dying, "I know", he replied. "Baby, if something happens to me, all I ask of you is to take good care of the girls," he agreed because he knew that they meant the world to me. I took a deep breath and whispered *to myself, okay Lord, I'm ready for whatever plan you have for me,* and I drifted off to sleep. The next morning, I woke up and looked around and said, *hey I'm still here, God had answered my prayer*. This trial showed me that God had a bigger plan for my life and that it just wasn't my time to go. "Thank You Jesus for allowing me to see another day!"

Two years passed by and I started having complications with my legs swelling, so I went to the doctor. They regulated my medicine and sent me home. Three days later

I had a stroke and then a seizure which landed me in the hospital for weeks. Eventually, I had to learn how to walk and talk all over again. Depression began to set in as I wanted to give up once again. I began to think that no one wanted me because I couldn't walk or talk, even though I was married and had the girls by my side I still felt unwanted.

I soon began rehab. It was frustrating because I had to depend on others to do everything for me. I would just sit and cry because I couldn't get well fast enough. I wanted to be up and about as I was before the stroke, but I had to realize that this too was only a test. A test of my faith. How much of it did I really have? Well time would only tell. The seizures would start for no apparent reason and was very scary. I could sometimes feel them coming on and often tried to control them but that wasn't always the case. I would go into a convulsion, shaking uncontrollably, eyes rolling, and mouth twisted and twitching, hyperventilation would set in, then, it all would pass. Sometimes this would happen several times back to back before it all would finally subside. I couldn't grasp the fact that I was wheelchair bound, eventually began to use a walker, then I graduated to the use of a cane, then nothing at all.

Depression had a permanent residence in me with all this sickness going on; I didn't know how much more I could take. I was spiraling downward. It was draining me physically and mentally with nowhere to turn as I began to cry, cutting my wrists, cutting my legs; this thing called depression really had me down. Devin immediately took me to the doctor and had me admitted in the hospital. From there I was transferred to the Psych Ward for a medical evaluation. I cried and cried begging Devin not to leave me. "Baby, I don't want to leave you, but you need to get help with this depression." I just sat there sobbing as he exited to door. For the next month, I was bound down in rehab for major depressive disorder. I went through a lot of group therapy, role playing, art sessions and one on one sessions with several psychologists and psychiatrists. The therapy was very intense, but I made it through it all because I was determined to overcome my past and present state.

Then, again I began to spiral downward-my mind and emotions were all over the place. I seriously felt as if I was really losing my mind. I knew that I needed help but I didn't want to seek the help that I needed because I was afraid that people would think that I was crazy, knowing that I wasn't, I was just depressed and didn't know how to handle it. To this day I still sometimes struggle with depression, it's a disease of your mind's thought process. You have to learn how to cope with it and everyday life to make it through. I do believe that some of my depression comes from my past relationship history and obstacles, not really knowing how to cope with my deep inner feelings. At one point I didn't know how to let go of the negative baggage and I brought it along with everything else in my life. I now realize that my present life has no place or space for the negative excess baggage.

Sometimes it's very hard to love family and sometimes family is the world's worst to deal with, but you handle the situation at hand the best way you know how. Wish them the best and move on with your life. In marriage, don't let your family dysfunctions trickle down into your new life and your new journey, because it can be destructive. To keep your sanity, you have to keep moving forward and not let your one dysfunctional family dictate the amazing person who you have grown to be, "Unglued". Continue to say, "I trust you Lord".

After all the doctor visits, all the rehab, all the praying, constantly battling depression and family dysfunction, I made it through these trials and tests, once again. This is a test to be someone's testimony, this is my story for someone else's glory. So, Lord, I trusted you for the mighty healing and thank you for making me whole again. My family needs me: I need you, so here I am Lord.

To anyone who has been through or going through depression and family dysfunction believe that you can overcome, and you can win. Even in your darkest times pray, trust, and believe that there is a higher power. God's got your back because He said He, would and He never ever fails.

"Become Unglued and Be Blessed"

XII
SIMPLY ME
(Reflections)

Looking Inside Myself and Surviving

I have been through some things in my life that I'm not proud of. I often find myself reflecting on how domestic violence, major disappointments and being the object of my cousin's hidden desires affected me in the past and in my adult life. I can honestly say the trauma affected me a great deal and caused me to be guarded about everything. I was once very uncomfortable with guys approaching me, looking at me, or even touching me because it would just take me back to that very dark place that I didn't want to ever go back to. I had to learn a lot of things on my own, not really having someone there to really teach me about life. I know that may be hard to believe from someone that was raised in a two-parent home. In my parent's home I was taught about the simple things in life, such as being respectful and providing for one's self. I didn't understand my life growing up as I know it now. Although I have siblings, two brothers and one sister ranging from two years to eighteen years apart, I really felt alone. With such a broad age range we didn't have that close-knit bond. My parents were very strict on me growing up, mainly because I was the only girl at the time, so it was rough. I couldn't do things with the other kids in the neighborhood, couldn't go certain places, and was shielded for most of my childhood life.

As a teenager, I didn't know a whole lot about boys, sex, or just socializing with people in general. It wasn't until I was much older that I was allowed to experience life as a teenager; and sometimes that was still hard. Growing up as "Simply Me" was just that. I was a simple individual, with a simple look, with a simple life. Being alone with no one to talk to, to share my thoughts, dreams and secrets with or even just to ask about the, what ifs of life. I remember when I first got my period; I was so scared I didn't know what to do. I was scared to tell my mother at first because we had never had the conversation before about becoming a young woman, so it was very scary for me; all I could see at the time was red. I didn't have a clue what a sanitary napkin or a tampon was, so clueless.

After finally telling my mother that I got my period, she began to tell me all that I needed to know from that point. I say to all young mothers out there, teach your daughters about becoming a young lady and all that is necessary for her to handle, so when the time comes, she won't be caught off guard. Educate her about becoming, the do's and don'ts about keeping herself clean and make sure that she's aware that her body is precious and sacred and to keep it protected at all cost. Advise her that boys will be boys and that teenage pregnancy is on the rise and that it's not an option.

As I journeyed through my "Simple" life I often dreamed of becoming someone important when I approached adulthood; a doctor a teacher even a flight attendant but somewhere along the way I will admit that I didn't make the best choices, but the choices I made at the time, I thought, were best for me. Now later in life I see that the choices that I made were indeed bad, but I realize now that I went through some tough junk in order to get to the good stuff. Suddenly my life went from "simple" to complicated with heartaches and many failed relationships, but I made it through. I have made mistakes in my life and sometimes I feel that I'm still paying for those mistakes, but you learn from those mistakes and move on with your life as you know it today. I have dealt with the choices that I have made in the past and now I have victory.

To all who have been violated by a relative or anyone else, whether it was sexually or other entities, just know that this behavior is not acceptable, it's a dysfunction and it's definitely a crime. It doesn't matter what your age is, never be afraid to cry out and seek for help, always stand up for yourself and let the perpetrator be known to any adult, someone who you trust, like a parent, teacher, counselor, neighbor and of course your local law enforcement. Get educated, and be aware of your surroundings, stay guarded at all times and always, always be safe.

No one is perfect, I live my life as I know it today, trying to keep peace among others, loving as I should and being as fair to others as I know how. I have made peace with it all. To everyone who have been inspired by this book, it's okay to be simple and victorious instead of being complicated and broken. Live the best life you know how because we only have oneself to deal with and that's our own. Love is Beautiful. Peace is always needed, and the struggle of life is REAL.

XIII

"SIMPLY ME"
My Passion &
My Purpose

I believe that everyone has something they can be passionate about. I believe that God has a greater purpose for us all. I have a heartfelt passion for helping everyone that I meet. Whatever they need at that time, whether it's a shoulder to cry on, words of encouragement or just good old fashion conversation; I am that person. I gravitate to people who are true to themselves and their immediate circumstances. I have a passion to always do what is right and to be fair to everyone.

I know what it feels like to work through your pain. I fought through my pain by praying, long conversations with my grandmother, obtaining guidance from my pastor and even talking to other people who were also going through. I believe that having compassion for others and giving valuable information will help them as they begin a positive path, just as I did. I am constantly giving encouragement to others assuring them that they too are not alone in their process of overcoming obstacles. It's not anyone's fault if they sometimes make bad choices, but the reality of it all is to learn from those bad choices and move forward and never look back.

Everyone has a Purpose. Find out what your Purpose in life is and make the proper adjustments according to that purpose. My purpose is to walk by faith not by sight. I also believe we should treat others how we want to be treated. God has brought me through many storms in my life thus far and I'm still standing to tell about His goodness. I have a Purpose to educate others about my life experiences and let them know that if I survived then they can too; there's always a way out.

My Purpose is to Endure Life's Storms

Storms will come and go. In the midst of the storm is where the test of your faith is. I have learned while going through my storms to stay prayerful and be true to myself.

My Purpose is to Motivate

Motivating one's self is continuing to work hard at whatever to do and be successful at it. To keep striving for continued excellence as we all excel through this thing called life

My Purpose is to Inspire

Encouraging others to aim high because the sky is the limit, it's not how high you go, it's how far you rise above it all.

My Purpose is to Love

There is space in everyone's life's journey for love, so choosing not to love is not an option. The good book states: love others as you love yourself.

A Purpose to Live

Whatever storm you're going through will become calm with the willingness to live. God gave us life as we know it with a purpose of having eternal life. Life is so precious. Love it and live it to the fullest.

Looking Inside Myself and Surviving

XIV

INSPIRATIONAL QUOTES
From My Heart

*Passages that represent the thoughts of the mind:
Sharing your experiences and visions boldly with others
allows you to speak softly from the heart.*

"Not once does the Bible say", "Worry about it",
"Stress over it", "Figure it out", But the BIBLE over
and over clearly says, 'Trust GOD'

"Beauty is an understanding of what you have, and it's
forgiving yourself of what you don't have and
appreciating all of it"

"A Moment of Pain is like...A lifetime of Glory"

Stay on the course and finish the race"

*"Some say that I can do anything,
Some say I'm better than I am,
But who is to say that I'm not?"*

"We do what we have to do ....To do what we want to do .... "Pray hard, study Hard" and work Hard. It all will pay off and eventually comes full circle

"God will put you where He wants you .... Even if no one thinks you deserve the position"

"I've battled my whole life to become the Strong Woman I am today. If you think you can take me down after all that I've already been through, give it your best shot. You will not succeed because I am one of God's chosen.

LORD,
Enlighten what's dark in me,
Strengthen what's weak in me,
Mend what's broken in me,
Bind what's bruised in me,
And lastly, revive whatever peace and love
That has died in me.
AMEN

Don't ever give up,
Don't ever give in,
Don't ever stop trying,
Don't ever sellout,
And if you find yourself succumbing to one of the above
for a brief moment
Pick yourself up,
brush yourself off,
Whisper a prayer and start where you left off;
But never ever give up!

"Our Loving Heavenly Father"
I have tried to hide these fears and worries. I don't know if others' can see through my smile, but I believe you know my heart. I come to you for help, please show

me what to do and give me the strength to do it, In JESUS loving name I pray. Amen

When the hand of God is on your life, sometimes it's hard to fit in.
You just can't do what everyone else does
"YOU HAVE BEEN CHOSEN FOR GREATER!"

*Heavenly Father,
Walk through my home and take away all my worries and any illnesses. Please watch over and heal my family and friends. Bless my home, family and friends with peace, love and joy. In Jesus name ………Amen!*

*Whatever you are facing today
Keep on praying
Keep on loving
Keep on hoping
Keep pressing on
There is Victory on the other side*

Never be ashamed of what you have been through
God will use your story for
His precious glory

"You may not understand today or tomorrow,
But eventually God will reveal why you went through
everything you did"

"Be patient ....Sometimes you have to go
through the worst to get to the best"

GOD has a purpose for your pain.
a reason for your struggles
and a gift for your faithfulness
Don't ever give up!

GOD is fighting your battles
Arranging things in your favor
And making a way
Even when you don't even see a way!
Eyes wide open.

*"The fact that you are still breathing,
Is proof that GOD has a greater purpose for you"*

*"Start where you are,
Use what you have,
And do all you can,
To be all that you were created to be"*

*Act like it is,
Even though it isn't,
In order that it might be,
"A Creation of Self"*

*"Embracing your inner beauty,
simply define who you are"*

*"Negativity and chatter clutter the mind,
Distance yourself so you can breathe
Discard old wounds from your past,
So you can receive a mended healing for your future*

*"If you think it, you can write it, then, you can.
Speak it into existence"*

*Don't follow in someone else's success,
Live within your own dreams and Success will follow*

*Believing in you is winning,
While unbelieving and doubt is losing*

*"Walk in your truth of who you are,
Not in doubt of who you could have been"*

*Walk in pride with your head held high, looking down
is not an option*

*Be proud of your heritage, God's creation of you
represents your ancestors that came before you*

Reach deep inside your soul and pull out all that God has for you

Success is an option. It's up to you to make it happen; The sky is the limit

Steering clear of your negative past allows you too continuously
strive for excellence, be patient; the best is yet to come

Weathering the storm is a constant struggle, but serving God with a clear conscious is a guaranteed victory

Protecting your heart is a fragile necessity, handle it with extreme care

Tears that flow out from deep within, often is good for the soul

As morning comes, the warmth of the rising sun awakens me, eyes wide open, so I suddenly began to smile, then cry tears of joy giving God all the praises for another day in this thing call Life; Another incredible opportunity to live

Positive motivation promotes a strong impact that influences the lives of others. Reach up, aim high and look past the negative and gain all that's positive for an impeccable future

A Blueprints of your life reflects the canvas of who you are

Be Honest, Be Courageous and Be Bold in your truth and in value of self.
Love yourself for who you are and be at peace in which you were created
Just Be You

"Create in you a clean heart, so that your Soul can shine in the presence of God"

"You have to be a positive role model within yourself, before you can be a positive role model to someone else; a positive imprint will leave a lasting impression"

"Paving the way down a crooked path can lead to greatness for others to follow"

Sometimes our minds are cloudy with clutter; let the rain flow to clear the air, then, you can smile

Be of good courage while believing in your passion, as you continue to inspire others when walking in your truth

3P's
Patience!

Passion!
Purpose!
"Be Patient, discover your Passion and grow in your Purpose"

Just because someone wants to clown, doesn't mean you have to join the circus.
Cash in your ticket and exit the gate

A genuine friendship is built on TRUST; don't devalue it by being fake"

God created everyone equal, but it's up to you to keep yourself level. Always strive for excellence and never settle for less in any true relationship, be in it for the long haul if there is an infinite connection. Commitment is a must, Vows are Sacred, and an intertwined Love is definitely real.

About Me

I was born Phyllis Marie Proctor in Waco, Texas to Clarence Sr. and Laura Mae Long-Proctor on October 19, 1965. I was raised on the eastside of town of Waco, Texas. I am the second to the oldest of four children. At the age of twelve, I gave my life to Christ, where I was brought up in the Baptist religion. I attended Waco Public Schools until I graduated in 1984 from Richfield High School. As I grew up, I worked hard to get what I wanted in life. I am a very independent individual with big visions and goals.

There are many activities that I enjoy including helping others, reading, writing, making new friends and most of all spending time with my family. These are just some of the things I am passionate about.

I have worked in the Criminal Justice System for twelve years. Working with at risk youth is another one of my passions. I often feel that if I can at least help one troubled youth to get on the right path in his or her life, then my ultimate goal will be accomplished, and my sense of purpose will be fulfilled.

I also volunteer at local Detention Centers; this has always been very inspirational and motivating for me. I love to make a difference in the lives of disadvantaged youth in the city and local community. They can always use positive uplifting and a positive role model. It is my belief that if I just offer an ear to listen as they express their feelings of self-doubt and rejection without being judged or misunderstood, I could help them discover their God given purpose. This is my "My Mission" and "My Purpose."

At the present time, I am a member of the United Methodist Church, where my very important mission is to help others. I take serving in the church very seriously. Currently, I serve as Usher Board President, Greeter Vice-Chair, Church Anniversary Co-Chair (2015), Church Council voting member, Church Finance Treasurer (2015-2016) and a Notary Public, certified by the State of Texas.

I am a small business owner as an Independent Beauty Consultant for Mary Kay Inc; I am a certified color and skincare specialist, where I have been voted Unit Miss Go Give, runner up in personal sales and Queen of Personal sales. In my spare time I enjoy praise dancing and spiritual miming.

In 1989, I married the love of my life, Dwayne Keith Ewing and to this union; we adopted two beautiful daughters, Kayla and Taylor Ewing and I'm now blessed with two grandchildren. All of this was just an Almighty Blessing from my GOD.

I am a "Virtuous Woman" who wears many hats with a purpose and a passion, and the Lord is not through with me yet.

Phyllis M. Ewing

For Booking

Author, Motivational Speaker- Phyllis Ewing is an advocate and survivor of Domestic Violence and Sexual Abuse. She is available to speak at your church, organization or any special event on the following topics:

- ❖ Sexual Abuse
- ❖ Domestic Abuse
- ❖ Infertility and Adoption
- ❖ Faith
- ❖ Overcoming Depression

For booking please contact her Publisher Dr. Sherrie Walton at admin@iamsherriewalton.com

www.ingramcontent.com/pod-product-compliance
Lightning Source LLC
Chambersburg PA
CBHW052055070526
44584CB00017B/2193